# 101 Property Tax Tips

## 2021/22

By

**Jennifer Adams**

**Publisher Details**

This guide is published by Tax Insider Ltd, 3 Sanderson Close, Warrington WA5 3LN. '101 Property Tax Tips' (formerly '101 Property Tax Secrets Revealed' and '101 Tax Tips for Landlords') first published in November 2012, second edition May 2013, third edition June 2014, fourth edition November 2015, fifth edition September 2016, sixth edition July 2019, seventh edition November 2020, eighth edition May 2021.

**Copyright**

A CIP Copy of this book is available from the British Library.

ISBN 978-1-9161577-4-3

**All rights reserved**

**Trademarks**

## Disclaimer

This guide is produced for general guidance only, and professional advice should be sought before any decision is made. Individual circumstances can vary and therefore no responsibility can be accepted by Tax Insider, the co-author, Jennifer Adams or the publisher Tax Insider Ltd for any action taken or any decision made to refrain from action by any readers of this guide.

Tax rules and legislation are constantly changing and therefore the information printed in this guide is correct at the time of writing — May 2021

Neither the authors nor Tax Insider Ltd offer financial, legal or investment advice. If you require such advice then we urge you to seek the opinion of an appropriate professional in the relevant field. We care about your success and therefore encourage you to take appropriate advice before you put any of your financial or other resources at risk. Don't forget, investment values can decrease as well as increase.

The content of this guide is for information only and all examples and numbers are for illustration. Professional advice should always be sought before undertaking any tax planning of any sort as individual circumstances vary and other considerations may have to be taken into account before acting.

To the fullest extent permitted by law Jennifer Adams and Tax Insider Ltd do not accept liability for any direct, indirect, special, consequential or other losses or damages of whatsoever kind arising from using this guide.

# Contents

# About This Guide

Property owners become landlords for a variety of reasons but one thing that they all have in common is the desire to maximise rental income profits and/or capital growth from their property investment.

Unfortunately the government believes that it should take some of that profit or gain in the way of tax such that all property owners, whether an individual, a company, a trust or personal representatives of an estate will, at some time or other, find themselves subjected to tax on that property.

However, there is much that can be done to save or at least reduce the amount of tax payable.

This easy to read guide reveals insider tax saving tips and strategies that are currently available so that the minimal amount of property tax is payable, regardless of whether you are landlord, a property developer or own the property as a main residence.

Due to the restrictive number of pages, this book can only show some areas where tax planning is possible. More 'Tax Tips' can be found in the monthly newsletters of Tax Insider, Property Tax Insider and Business Tax Insider as well as on the Tax Insider website.

It must be stressed that professional advice should always be sought when undertaking any form of tax planning.

# Chapter 1.
# Different Ways Of Owning Property

1. Private Landlord

2. Corporate Or LLP Landlord

3. 'Special Purpose Vehicle' Companies

4. Management Company

5. Trader Or Investor?

6. Change In Type Of Ownership

7. Methods Of Personal Ownership

8. Profit Allocation

9. Joint Spouse/Civil Partnership Ownership (1)

10. Joint Spouse/Civil Partnership Ownership (2)

11. Joint Non-Spouse/Civil Partnership Ownership

# 1.    Private Landlord

The vast majority of UK properties are privately owned by individuals, many having been purchased as an investment rather than as a main residence.

The private investor landlord is taxed on the amount of letting income received less allowable expenses incurred on a fiscal year basis, as well as on any capital gain that may be made on the sale. Inheritance tax may be payable on the value of the property held at the date of death. Stamp Duty Land Tax (Land and Buildings Transaction Tax in Scotland, Land Transaction Tax in Wales) may be payable on the purchase of the property and VAT may be due if the business is trading.

Individuals who purchase property jointly, intending to rent for the long term are taxed on their share of the annual rental profits and/or any gains made on sale. Joint owners of property purchased with the intention to sell after restoration are likely to be in a 'trading partnership' with each being taxed as a self-employed 'property dealer' which could mean becoming liable to National Insurance contributions.

For a 'trading' partnership to exist there needs to be a degree of organisation with a view to making a profit (similar to that required for an ordinary commercial business). A partnership agreement is, therefore, recommended.

If the landlord has no other income, the annual personal allowance is deducted from any profit made on the letting income in full. If he or she has other income, the personal allowance either may not be available or be restricted such that any profits made will be taxed at the landlord's marginal rate of tax.

A 'Property Allowance' is available to individual landlords, the claiming of which removes the liability to tax should gross rental income be less than £1,000 (see Tip 33). Where gross income is more than £1,000, the

3

allowance can be deducted in place of the actual expenses amount where this produces a lower taxable profit. This will obviously be the situation where the expenses are less than £1,000. However, actual expenses should be deducted where this produces a loss in order to preserve that loss.

Depending upon the level of letting profit, being a sole investor could be more expensive in comparison with joint investor ownership. A sole investor will be taxed in full at his or her marginal rate of tax whereas, with joint investor ownership, the letting profit is split with each owner's share of the profit being taxed at his or her respective marginal rate. It will all depend on the tax rates of each respective investor.

For example, should a property be jointly owned 50:50 and one taxpayer be a basic rate taxpayer and the other a higher or additional rate taxpayer, the total tax bill will be reduced by 50% of the difference between the tax due at the higher and lower rates as compared with the tax that would be payable were the income received solely by the higher or additional rate taxpayer. Further tax reduction is possible should one investor be a non-taxpayer, as the full amount of that individual's personal allowance will be available for offset.

If the taxpayer is a basic rate taxpayer and the property has been put in joint names where one partner was a higher rate or additional rate taxpayer then the tax bill will increase.

**Practical Point**

The default split of joint ownership between husband and wife is 50:50. However, if it is more income tax efficient for the split to be different, then the profit may be divided according to actual underlying ownership of the property (if different and tax efficient) once HMRC has been notified (see Tips 9 and 10).

The example that follows shows the tax position should one spouse be taxed at a higher tax rate from the other.

## Private Landlord

Joanne and Robert are married and jointly own a portfolio of rental properties 50:50.

For the year 2021/22 each has other income such that Joanne is a 20% basic rate taxpayer but Robert is a 45% additional rate taxpayer.

Total net rental profit is £825 per month, i.e. £9,900 per year = £4,950 each.

Joanne: Tax liability of £990 (£4,950 @ 20%).

Robert: Tax liability of £2,227.50 (£4,950 @ 45%).

If Robert owned the properties as a sole investor then the tax liability would be £4,455; by owning the properties jointly with Joanne, there is a tax saving of £1,237.50.

This saving could be increased should the properties be solely in Joanne's name assuming that the taxable profit does not take her into the higher rate tax band. However, should Robert not want to relinquish full ownership he could give Joanne say, 5% submit a form 17 to HMRC and be taxed on the underlying properties of ownership, 95% being taxed at basic rate and 5% at higher rates. (see Tips 9 and 10).

# 2.    Corporate Or LLP Landlord

## Company limited by shares

There are different types of companies but the one most commonly used for property tax planning is the private company limited by shares. Shareholders are the owners of the company, which is administered by directors (who may also be the shareholders). There are advantages and disadvantages of a company owning property for example, although companies do not have a personal allowance, if the profits from a property business owned by individual(s) are charged at the higher personal tax rates, it could potentially be more beneficial for the properties to be owned by a company. At 19% the corporation tax rate is lower than tax rates charged to an individual. However, once this tax has been paid, there may be further tax costs should the shareholder make withdrawals as dividends as well as additional compliance costs.

Another beneficial difference is that on a personal gain the tax has to be paid within 30 days of completion of the sale (see Tip 55 whereas for a company the gain is included in the calculation of profit or loss with any tax being payable nine months and one day after the accounting period end.

Further, tax relief on interest paid on loans by individual property investors is restricted such that the amount paid only attracts tax relief at the basic rate charge of 20% as an income tax reduction. These rules do not apply to interest on loans incurred by companies (see Tip 19).

Other relevant points:

- A limited company is a separate legal entity from the shareholders.

- Profits and losses belong to the company.

- The company can continue regardless of the death, resignation or bankruptcy of the shareholders or directors (although there must be at least one director in place).

- The liability of shareholders is limited to the amount unpaid (if any) on the shares held.

- If the company fails, the shareholders are not normally required to make good the deficit (unless personal guarantees have been given).

- A company may find it easier to raise finance.

Most investors operate their property business either as a 'private landlord' or as a company.

**Limited Liability Partnership**

In some cases, operating via a Limited Liability Partnership (LLP) may be preferable. Profits of an LLP are divided amongst the partners (owners) and then taxed at the marginal rate of each partner. The benefit is that the partnership profit split can be changed year on year if required and a different split is tax beneficial – unlike as for companies or personal ownership.

The individual partners are treated as being self-employed, paying income tax on their share of the profits, and Class 2 and Class 4 National Insurance Contributions, where relevant. An LLP can acquire property or the partners can transfer property that they already own into the LLP. Transferring property into the LLP can be advantageous from a tax perspective. The property is held on trust but the underlying legal ownership remains unchanged, therefore no SDLT or CGT is payable on the transfer. Where a member transfers property into the LLP, the value of that property at the time of transfer forms the opening balance on their equity account.

# 3.    'Special Purpose Vehicle' Companies

A Special Purpose Vehicle ('SPV') company is a company created for a specific purpose. A property SPV is created specifically to hold property that is being developed. Once the development has been completed, the properties sold and the lenders paid, the company is placed into liquidation (usually with the benefit of CGT Business Asset Disposal Relief (see Tip 58) and a new company formed for the next project.

SPVs are not necessarily used for tax planning purposes but to isolate financial risk, protecting a project from operational or insolvency issues; they can also be used to create joint ventures that protect partners from risk. However, many more landlords are now purchasing rental property via an SPV limited company because it can be more tax efficient now that the changes to tax relief on finance costs for individual landlords are fully in place (see Tip 19).

In comparison, a company is allowed to offset all mortgage interest against rents receive when calculating its corporation tax. Corporation tax is also at the lower rate of 19% in comparison with personal higher rates of tax although of course a company does not have a personal allowance.

The problem for serial SPV developers is that incorporating and closing a company in relatively quick succession could be seen by HMRC as being 'phoenixing' which is subject to Targeted Anti-Avoidance Rules. These rules were enacted to ensure that anyone closing a limited company and then opening a new one in the same trade would have to seek non-statutory clearance with HMRC. This enables HMRC to check that the winding up of the company is for genuine reasons and not for the sole purpose of gaining a tax advantage.

One way to alleviate the possibility of such a claim is to leave at least two years between the closure of one property development SPV and the start of the next or (more usually) by setting up subsidiary companies to create a group structure so that the assets are ring-fenced, even if the parent company goes bankrupt, or vice versa.

Once the property has been sold any after-tax profits in the SPV can be drawn into the holding company without any further tax charge and the SPV can then be wound up. A new subsidiary of the holding company is then formed for the next deal and the process repeated as often as necessary for each successive project until final closure, at which point the whole structure is wound up and profits extracted as capital.

# 4. Management Company

A higher rate taxpayer landlord taxed at 40% (or 45% if an 'additional rate' taxpayer) may be able to achieve some benefit from the lower 19% rate of corporation tax whilst still retaining ownership of the properties by incorporating a company that collects the rental income on behalf of the landlord.

Under this arrangement a set amount is deducted from the rental income received into the company's bank account as a management charge for the service role of managing the property business. The balance of income is paid to the landlord as rental income.

There will be few claimable expenses as what expenses are allowable will relate to the actual running of the management company (e.g. stationary, phone bill, salary). Corporation tax will be payable on any profit and any withdrawals will be as dividends, preferably of amounts that allow the dividend not to be subject to the higher rates of personal dividend tax.

The management/service charge is then a fully allowable expense against the rental income received in the hands of the landlord.

It has been suggested that a landlord can only benefit from this form of tax planning if they own at least four or five properties as the cost of preparation and additional compliance of a company is higher than for a sole trader/property investor.

However, the point should be made that the higher the number of properties, the higher the management charge and consequently the higher the tax relief thereon for a personal investor taxed at higher rates in comparison with using a company.

There will be a 'one off' legal fee on the setting up of the management company and increased administration thereafter and therefore a proper agreement between the company and the owner is advised. Legal fees are tax deductible against the management service charge received.

# 5.    Trader Or Investor?

Anyone buying a property to let out on a long-term basis will most likely be deemed an investor, whereas someone buying to refurbish then sell, whether resulting in a gain or not, could by HMRC to be deemed as trading or dealing in properties and be taxed accordingly.

The two factors to consider are intention (the reason for the purchase) and whether the transaction has the characteristics of being a trade. If it can be shown that the property has been purchased for its income, then the fact that it was sold as a result of getting a good offer shortly afterwards for example, need not convert the transaction into one of being a trade.

In deciding whether the transaction is a trade HMRC will refer to what are termed the 'Badges of Trade' using the same headings as when determining whether a self assessment business is a 'trade'.

Benefits of being deemed a 'trading' activity rather than 'investment' include:

• the use of losses is more varied;

• pension contributions are possible as such contributions require relevant earnings.

In addition, the outright sale of a trading business (rather than individual assets) would usually be eligible for Business Asset Disposal Relief (see Tip 58), where the gain is taxed at 10% on the first £1 million of eligible gain made in a lifetime rather than the investment tax charge of 20% if a higher rate taxpayer.

A particular problem may arise for those engaged in the property business in some way (e.g. a builder, surveyor or estate agent). Even though the purchase itself may have nothing to do with their trade HMRC could try to argue that the purchase of land and subsequent sale is a trading transaction.

## Trader or Investor?

In the case of *Kirkby v Hughes* (1992) BTC 52 Mr Kirkby was a builder who also developed property. He bought a property, carried out improvements, lived in it for a while and then sold it.

He tried to claim that the property was his main residence and as such exempt from capital gains tax. HMRC and the tribunal disagreed and found that he was trading.

It was held that because he was already a builder, he had to go further and prove that he was occupying the property as his main residence to be exempt from tax. As such the burden of proof was greater on him than for other taxpayers.

# 6.     Change In Type Of Ownership

- **A trading property becomes an investment property**

Such a situation may arise should a developer buy a plot of land with a view to building houses and selling at a profit but following completion not all are sold. If the developer decides to keep these remaining properties indefinitely for rent, then they are no longer deemed trading stock but become a fixed asset in the accounts. Unfortunately the tax rules will treat the developer as if he had sold these houses to himself for their market value producing a Capital Gains Tax (CGT) charge but having no profits out of which to pay the tax. The only way to reduce the tax bill in such a situation would be to identify any such investment properties at as an early a stage of the development as possible so that the profit on which the tax will be paid is based on as low a value as possible.

- **Investment properties becoming trading properties**

Should the opposite situation occur there will still be a deemed disposal for CGT purposes, but this time it will be possible to elect to 'hold over' (i.e. 'defer') the profit. This will mean that no immediate CGT is payable until the property or business is sold. In the trading accounts the property will be shown at original cost (termed 'appropriation to trading stock'). As such, any future profit on sale will be taxed as income.

If the property is owned individually, it might be possible to transfer the investment property into a developer/ trading company (e.g. 'Special Purpose Vehicle' - see Tip 3) so that on sale the tax liability will be lower at corporate tax rates than at personal tax rates. This process also means that any gain on sale could be eligible for Business Asset Disposal Relief (see Tip 58) or Business Property Relief for inheritance tax (see Tip 88).

As much evidence as possible to confirm intention will be needed in case HMRC query the planning.

# 7.    Methods Of Personal Ownership

Persons who own property on their own do so in their sole name with sole rights.

The two ways by which property may be held jointly are either as:

• Joint tenants – where each owner has equal rights over the property such that when one dies the property is automatically transferred into the other owner's name or

• Tenants in common – where each owner's share is separate, they may be unequal and may be disposed of in the owner's lifetime or on death as the respective owner wishes.

Spouses/civil partners can own property in their own names or jointly, but usually do so as joint tenants.

Two or more unmarried persons may own property either as joint tenants or tenants in common, although it is more usual for the ownership to be as tenants in common.

Joint owners need not own the property equally 50:50 but in whatever proportion is desired. Any change in proportion will incur legal costs should the original purchase be as equal joint tenants and a different split is required. Amending the underlying percentage ownership may be tax efficient (see Tips 9 and 10).

# 8.    Profit Allocation

The rental profit or loss incurred on a property held jointly (or held within a partnership business proper) need not be allocated in the same proportion as the underlying ownership. The owners can agree on a different split as they see fit, the proportion referring to profits and losses only and not necessarily to the underlying proportion of ownership.

Spouses and civil partners are deemed to own a property equally 50:50 unless they elect to be taxed according to the underlying ownership (see Tips 9 and 10). Further information and calculations can be found in HMRC's Property Income Manual Section 1030.

## Profit Allocation

The purchase deed of 54 Dorchester Place shows that the property ownership is split 90:10 between John and his partner, Jacinthe. For the tax year 2021/2022, the net rental profit is £13,200 per year. John is a 40% higher rate taxpayer whilst Jacinthe is a student with no income other than her share of the profit.

John's annual tax bill is £4,752 on his 90% share (£13,200 x 90% @ 40%); Jacinthe has no tax to pay on her 10% share of £1,320 (£13,200 x 10%), as this amount is less than the personal allowance for the year. Joint net amount remaining after tax = £13,200 – £6,072 = £7,128.

It would be more beneficial for the 99:1 split to be in Jacinthe's favour as this would mean a lower tax bill for John of £528 (£13,200 x 10% @ 40%) and nil for Jane. Joint net amount remaining after tax = £13,200 – £528 = £12,672.

There would be a tax saving of £4,224.

# 9.    Joint Spouse/Civil Partnership Ownership (1)

By default, rental profit from property jointly owned by spouses/civil partners is taxed 50:50 irrespective of the underlying respective proportion of actual ownership (this does not apply to property held within a business partnership proper or to commercial letting of furnished holiday accommodation).

However, if it would be more income tax efficient for the split of profit to be different, then the profit may be divided according to actual ownership, no formal election being required. A couple may change the underlying ownership to suit but note that such unequal ownership can be achieved only if the property is held as 'tenants in common' (see Tip 7).

A Form 17 *'Declaration of beneficial interest in joint property and income'* must be filed with HMRC within 60 days of the date of its signature (this restriction is strictly applied) together with evidence of the respective beneficial interests (e.g. the signing of a declaration of trust or a deed of arrangement).

A Form 17 is purely a declaration of interest for tax purposes and comes into effect from the date of signature (i.e. it cannot be back dated) and it remains in place until a replacement form is submitted. It cannot be used to change the income split back to 50:50 unless either the interests in the property or income change, or the owners stop living together as a married couple/civil partners or one of the joint owners' dies.

Even the smallest change in interest cancels the declaration and without submission of a subsequent form, the 50:50 split will apply automatically. On death or permanent separation, the income is split as to the beneficial interest.

## Joint Spouse/Civil Partnership Ownership (1)

Andrew and Anne are married and jointly own a rented property.

Andrew is a 45% additional rate taxpayer and Anne is a 20% basic rate taxpayer. Their accountant has calculated that it would be more beneficial for the profit to be split 80:20 to ensure that the least income tax is paid.

The legal ownership was changed to 80:20 held as 'tenants in common' and the declaration Form 17 signed, but unfortunately the form was not submitted within the 60-day time limit.

The income tax split therefore remains at 50:50 but legally the underlying ownership has changed to 80:20. The 50:50 tax split will remain until a fresh Form 17 is submitted.

Note: the legal fees for such a change will be at least £2,000 so the income tax saving must ensure to be less than this amount.

# 10.   Joint Spouse/Civil Partnership Ownership (2)

If one spouse/civil partner owns a rental property solely in their own name but is a higher or additional rate taxpayer and the other spouse/civil partner is not, it would be beneficial for at least some of the rental profit to be taxed on the spouse/civil partner.

To alter the income tax percentage charged, ownership of part of the property must be transferred into the other spouse/civil partner's name.

Should the owning spouse/civil partner not wish to transfer any material percentage ownership but still wish to reduce their tax bill, a nominal amount of, say, 1% could be transferred.

In this instance the HMRC Form 17 *'Declaration of beneficial interest in joint property and income'* (see Tip 9) must not be signed because not signing will ensure that the underlying property ownership is (say) 99:1 but the income split is 50:50.

## Joint Spouse/Civil Partnership Ownership (2)

Andrew and Anne are married. Andrew owns a property yielding

£8,000 rental income annually. Andrew is a 45% additional rate taxpayer and Anne is a non-taxpayer.

Andrew transfers 1% of the property ownership to Anne, retaining 99%.

Not submitting a form 17 will ensure that each is taxed on 50% of the income.

As Anne is a non-taxpayer, this transfer of 1% will produce a tax saving of **£1,800** (50% x £4,000 x 45%).

## 11.   Joint Non-Spouse/Civil Partnership Ownership

If a property is jointly owned by two persons who are not married or not in a civil partnership, the rental profit is not automatically split 50:50. Rather, the split is in whatever proportion they agree between themselves although the default position is in relation to the underlying ownership shares. The HMRC Form 17 *'Declaration of beneficial interest in joint property and income'* (see Tip 9) is not relevant in this instance but a written agreement would be helpful.

However, care is needed in making such arrangements. Should the owner wish to transfer rental income to someone else whilst retaining actual ownership (e.g. a parent may wish to pass on rental income to adult children to help them to save towards buying a property of their own), HMRC may try to enforce the 'settlements' anti-avoidance rules and tax the transferor owner. This challenge will be made even more probable if the owner can benefit from the property interest gifted (e.g. if the property interest is gifted on condition that the adult child returns the property interest to the parent after a fixed time period) or if the child is a minor.

If the parent wishes to transfer the right to a proportion of rental income instead of a share of the actual property, such an arrangement is potentially 'caught' by income tax anti-avoidance legislation regarding 'transfers of income streams'. This legislation applies where a right to 'relevant receipts' (which could include rental income) is transferred to another person without a transfer of the asset (i.e. the property) from which the income arises.

# Chapter 2.
# Letting Accounts

12.  Record Keeping

13.  Making Tax Digital

14.  Basis Of Assessment

15.  Property Deposits

16.  'Duality Of Purpose'

17.  Car Expenses

18.  Legal Fees

19.  Loan Interest Restriction

20.  Unrelieved Mortgage Interest

21.  Extracting Capital

22.  Portfolio Mortgages

23.  Loan Finance Costs

24.  Repairs

25.  'Replacement Furniture' Relief

26.  Pre-Letting Expenses

27.  Pre-Letting Repairs

28.  Post-Letting Expenses

29.  Expenses On Cessation

30.  Expenses On Sale

31.  Property Let At Less Than Market Rate

32.  'Rent-A-Room' Relief

33.  Property Allowance

34.  Furnished Holiday Lettings

# 12.  Record Keeping

UK-resident landlords are generally taxed on rental profits made wherever the properties are situated in the world. Non UK resident landlords of UK properties being taxed on UK rental income only (see Chapter 5).

A record of the rental income, expenses incurred, and capital items purchased must be kept. Separate sets of records are needed if the properties are let as 'furnished holiday lets' because these properties are taxed under different tax rules (see Tip 34). Properties owned by the same persons form a single rental business as do non-UK- owned properties and as such separate records are required.

**Keep:**

- invoices, expense and capital items, receipts, rental statements, mortgage statements;

- past years' income and expenditure accounts and Tax Returns submitted;

- bank statements;

- details of purchase of the property – date of acquisition, purchase price including associated costs;

- details of subsequent improvement costs; and

- if the property was previously the landlord's main residence, details of periods when the landlord lived in the property and of periods let – to ensure Principal Private Residence (see Chapter 7) are correctly claimed on sale.

**NOTES:**

- In the Tribunal case of *Ridpath* (*Ridpath v HMRC (2013) UKFTT89*) it was accepted that a total of £40,000 had likely been incurred on property improvements. However, the claim was disallowed because it was impossible to define precisely how much had actually been spent as there was no proof of the expenditure.

- HMRC have an index of the record-keeping requirements for a business available on the GOV.UK website at www.gov.uk/keeping-your-pay-tax-records/rental-income.

- A penalty of up to £3,000 can be imposed by HMRC for failure to maintain adequate records for self-assessment purposes.

### Record Keeping

Currently records can be kept manually, using spreadsheets or software packages. However, following the implementation of Making Tax Digital submissions will be required in digital format (see Tip 13).

HMRC accredited software packages include:

- Landlords Property Manager

  www.propertyportfoliosoftware.co.uk

- Landlord Vision

  www. landlordvision.co.uk

# 13.    Making Tax Digital

HMRC are undergoing a process of change directly relating to record keeping named 'Making Tax Digital' (MTD) under which taxpayers will be able to view and manage their tax information in one place via an online digital account. Each taxpayer will also be able to view their current ('real time') tax liabilities whichever type of tax is paid.

One of the most important requirements of MTD is that the records must be kept digitally; HMRC has confirmed that 'digitally' can mean via a spreadsheet.

In addition, the annual tax return submission is to be replaced by quarterly filing (termed 'an update') plus a final 'end of year activity' submission. When an 'update' is submitted, HMRC will calculate the taxpayer's potential tax bill in as close to 'real time' as possible and at the same time remind ('prompt') the taxpayer of the dates of payment. No changes are being made to the underlying tax rules, or the level of data required or dates of tax payment.

MTD is being introduced in stages with compulsorily VAT registered business taxpayers (including companies) having already joined the process. As from 6 April 2023 MTD will apply to all self-employed, partnerships and landlords (including trusts which receive income from property) whose combined gross income from those sources exceeds £10,000. Those taxpayers with combined income from all sources of less than £10,000 will be exempt.

The £10,000 turnover figure is the income from the properties and not the profit figure. If the landlord has an employment as well as rental income, then the employment income will count towards the £10,000.

**Number of submissions**

MTD regulations state that individual landlords must submit separate quarterly 'updates' for each property business category (i.e. separate 'updates' for lettings, furnished holiday lets and overseas lets). The minimum number of submissions will be five per tax year but depending upon the taxpayers' level and different types of income there could be as many as 20 submissions required.

**Practical Point**

For more information on the implications of MTD see the Tax Insider publication 'Making Tax Digital for Landlords'.

# 14.   Basis Of Assessment

As part of HMRC's intended 'Making Tax Digital' strategy (see Tip 13) where an individual landlords' annual turnover (gross rents) is less than £150,000, the default accounting method is now the cash basis. Companies and Limited Liability Partnerships are required to use the 'accrual' basis of accounting (i.e. recognise the income received, and expenses paid on an invoice basis, regardless of whether or when the cash is received).

However, an individual landlord can 'opt out' of the cash basis and use the 'accruals' basis by making an election on his or her tax return. It needs to be remembered that this election will only take the landlord out of the cash basis for one tax year and will have to be made for each subsequent year if required. This is done by ticking a box on the Property pages of the tax return.

When a landlord enters or leaves the cash basis, transitional rules are needed to adjust for accrued income and expenses and payments in advance. This ensures that all income and expenditure is accounted for only once.

Where the landlord has separate property businesses (e.g. one letting UK properties and another letting overseas properties), he/she can opt out of the cash basis for one property business and remain within for the other.

Where a property business is jointly owned by individuals who are not married to each other, each individual owner can independently decide whether to opt out or not. Should one decide to opt in and the other not then accounts for the property business are drawn up twice - once using the 'accruals' basic of accounting and another set using the cash basis. Where the property business is owned by a married couple/ civil partners, both individuals must either use the cash basis, or both the 'accruals' basis.

Partnerships can use the cash basis for a property business but only where all the partners are individuals. Companies, Limited Liability Partnerships, trustees and personal representatives are not permitted to use the cash basis for property businesses.

Where a property is let through a letting agent, HMRC consider that for the cash basis the date of receipt is the date that the letting agent receives the money from the tenant of the landlord's behalf, not the date on which the landlord receives the rent from the agent.

## Basis Of Assessment

Tony owns three properties in the UK, which he rents out. His rental income is £50,000 a year. He also owns a number of properties in Paris and Madrid, in respect of which he receives rental income of £200,000 a year. Tony and his wife Shirley jointly own a flat in the UK from which they receive rental income of £10,000 a year.

The cash basis will be the default basis for the UK properties, unless Tony chooses to opt out. By contrast, he will have to use the accruals basis for the overseas property business as the rental income exceeds the cash basis ceiling of £150,000.

The cash basis will also be the default for the jointly owned flat, unless both Tony and Shirley decide to opt out.

# 15.    Property Deposits

The usual practice when letting a property is for a tenant to pay a security deposit to a landlord before moving into the property. The deposit is returned at the end of the tenancy, subject to any deductions for 'dilapidations', i.e. any repairs that the tenant has not undertaken although is contractually obliged to do so.

On payment, the deposit is held on the tenant's behalf, the landlord having no legal right over the deposit money; he or she is only entitled to some or all of the deposit at the end of the tenancy.

Under the default cash basis rules, there is no requirement to account for the deposit when received. The landlord will only need to account for any element of the security deposit which is retained once it has been established that the retained element is legally the landlord's property.

Should the income be taxed under the 'accrual basis' rules, the tax position is that a deposit is income to be included in the letting accounts. However, the inclusion is deferred until the landlord acquires the right to retain some or all of the deposit, which is usually at the end of the tenancy. It is at that point that the amount of deposit retained is brought into the accounts as income and the cost of repair as an expense.

The repair costs may be greater than the deposit. In this situation, the tenant may pay the landlord compensation in addition to the amount of deposit. This additional amount is treated as income if the landlord subsequently re-lets the property. However, should the landlord not subsequently re-let then the payment is treated as a capital receipt.

# 16.  Duality Of Purpose

Expenses incurred in the running of a property letting business are deductible from rental income received in calculating the taxable profit. However, just because a payment has been made does not necessarily mean that it will be allowable.

Strictly, for an expense to be allowed the business purpose must be the sole purpose; there must be no dual reason for the expense. Where it is difficult to split the business element from any private element then the whole expense amount is usually disallowed.

In practice, however, some 'dual purpose'-type expenses may be permitted. The expense usually quoted is of expenses incurred on the running of a car used partly for business and partly for private purposes, the business part obviously being allowed (see Tip 17).

The cost of business-related travel in attending to rental properties is allowable as an expense for tax purposes, any travel costs incurred for personal reasons are not.

Travel costs in attending foreign let property can also be claimed again providing that there is no 'duality of purpose' (i.e. a visit is made to the property at the same time as being on holiday).

# 17.   Car Expenses

The cost of running a vehicle used in an unincorporated letting business can be claimed against rental income. Unless the vehicle is used solely for business purposes, the costs must be apportioned between private and business use.

There are two alternative methods of calculation:

1.   Note the recorded mileage on 6 April each year giving the total mileage over the full tax year. Record the mileage of every business-related trip made in the tax year, which will give the proportion of running costs to claim.

2.   Claim 45p for the first 10,000 business miles incurred and 25p for any additional miles, the ''simplified expenses' claim.

Under the 'simplified expenses' rules the claim uses a flat rate for mileage instead of claiming for the actual costs of buying and running the car.

A 'simplified expenses' claim cannot be made for a vehicle on which capital allowances have been claimed under the 'accrual' basis of assessment or for which the purchase cost has been claimed in accounts using the 'cash basis'. All individual landlords with income below £150,000 are required to use the 'cash' basis unless they claim to 'opt out'.

Whichever method is chosen, once used, it cannot be changed until the vehicle itself is changed.

## Car Expenses

James travels 12,000 miles on business attending to his portfolio of properties. The total recorded mileage (including private journeys) for the year is 15,000. Total cost of running the car is £3,750 per year.

Method 1: £3,750 x 12,000/15,000 = £3,000.

Method 2: (10,000 x 45p) + (2,000 x 25p) = £5,000.

Method 2 will produce the most tax-efficient amount to claim.

If the property owner is a company and the company owns the car that an employee (including a director if salaried) uses in the business then the usual PAYE benefit in kind company car scale rate rules apply. If the employee uses his/her own car in the business and the company usually gives the employee a mileage allowance to cover the cost; if the mileage allowance paid is greater than the mileage allowance amounts given above then any balance is taxed under PAYE.

Companies use the 'accruals' basis by default and can claim capital allowances on the purchase of the car.

# 18.　Legal Fees

Expenditure on professional fees is deductible from rental income as revenue expenditure for calculating the taxable profit if incurred for the purposes of the rental business. Fees incurred in relation to the purchase and/or sale of a property are tax deductible as capital expenditure on disposal of the property in the capital gains tax calculation.

Revenue items such as legal fees are deductible regardless of whether they are prepared under the 'cash' or 'accruals' basis, although the timing of the relief differs. Under the cash basis, the deduction is given for the period in which the expenditure incurred whereas for the 'accrual' basis relief is given for the period for which the expenditure relates (see Tip 14).

For capital expenditure different rules apply. No deduction is allowed for capital expenditure under the accrual basis, whereas it is deductible under the cash basis, unless the expenditure is of a type for which a deduction is expressly forbidden. Such expenses include expenditure in or in connection with lease premiums and the provision, alteration or disposal of land (including property).

No relief is available for abortive legal fees e.g. when attempting but failing to buy a property.

**Specific legal costs allowed as revenue expenditure incurred:**

- on the renewal of a lease if the lease is for less than 50 years (except for any proportion that relates to the payment of a premium on the renewal of a lease);

- in connection with the first letting if it is for less than a year (includes the cost of drawing up the lease, agents' and surveyors' fees and commission);

- on preparation of a replacement short lease where it closely follows a previous agreement;

- in relation to rent arbitration and evicting of an unsatisfactory tenant so the property can be re-let.

**Specific legal costs allowed as capital expenditure incurred:**

- generally, if the costs relate to a capital item e.g. the purchase or sale of a property;

- in connection with the first letting or subletting for more than one year (includes the cost of drawing up the lease, agents' and surveyors' fees and commission);

- if the property is put to other use between lets, or a long lease replaces a short lease.

# 19.   Loan Interest Restriction

Landlords are able to deduct loan interest and related costs from rental income in arriving at the taxable profit. However, the amount available on residential lets by a personal landlord is restricted such that only basic rate relief can be claimed as a tax credit as from 2021/22.

The tax reduction applies to each property business separately such that any 'excess' tax reduction on an overseas property business cannot be used against a UK property business or share of partnership property business or vice versa, for example.

The reduction is on the lower of the interest amount affected, the rental profits, and the individual's income (excluding savings and dividend income) for the tax year.

The amount claimable is further restricted to the market value of the property at the time when it was first let if originally not purchased with a view to rent. This reduction applies before any reduction in mortgage relief.

The rules do not apply to furnished holiday lets (see Tip 34), the profits of which adopt many of the trading calculation rules and therefore interest payments are allowable in full. They also do not affect landlords with commercial properties or those properties held within a company structure (see Tip 2).

## Loan Interest Restriction

Tony has a buy-to-let residential property portfolio from which he receives rental income of £60,000 a year. Mortgage interest is £20,000 a year and there are other deductible costs of £5,000 a year. On the assumption that his other income utilises the personal allowance and basic rate band, the property income is taxed at the 40% higher rate tax.

|  | 2021/22 |
| --- | --- |
| Rental income | £60,000 |
| Other expenses | (£5,000) |
| Mortgage interest | 0 |
| Taxable profit | £55,000 |
| Tax @ 40% | £22,000 |
| Tax reduction | (£4,000)* |
| Tax payable | £18,000 |
| Amount retained: After tax, expenses and mortgage paid | £17,000 |

*(£55,000 - £18,000) £20,000 x 20%

# 20.  Unrelieved Loan Interest

The amount of tax deduction that landlords with residential properties are able to claim on loan interest paid is restricted to the basic rate of tax (see Tip 19). Any amount not utilised in one year is carried forward to be added to the loan interest figure of the following year. The tax reduction is then calculated using both the balance of interest not utilised brought forward plus the current year's loan interest.

If a loss has been made then no tax deduction will be given and the unused finance cost amount for that year is carried forward and utilised in the following year's calculations.

The basic rate reduction/tax credit is 'capped' at the lower of the:

• finance costs not deducted in the tax year;

• profits of the business for the tax year; o r

• adjusted total income that exceeded the personal allowance for the year.

Any part of the disallowed interest not used is carried forward to subsequent years.

Should the tax reduction be less than the tax liability, it is capped at that liability, so as to reduce the tax bill to nil. The tax reduction cannot be used to create a tax refund.

## Unrelieved Loan Interest

John purchased a rental flat in September 2018. He has other income such that his allowances are used elsewhere. As at 6 April 2021 there was interest that has not been utilised in previous years brought forward of £7,500 and a loss brought forward of £(500).

For the year 2021/22, again his allowances were used elsewhere. The rent was £20,000, with expenses of £3,800 and mortgage interest of £6,000 all of which being available as tax credit. This creates a profit of £16,200 (i.e. income £20,000 - £3,800) less the loss brought forward of £(500).

There is also the brought forward disallowed interest of £7,500 to take into consideration which, when added to the interest amount of £6,000 produces total interest available to tax credit of £13,500.

This total amount of interest is the amount available as a tax credit for 2021/22 but restricted to the lower of the:

- disallowed interest - 20% of £13,500 = £2,700;

- property profits - 20% of £15,700 = £3,140;

- adjusted taxable income - £20,000 - £3,800 = £16,200.

Therefore the amount claimable for 2021/22 is £2,700 with the balance of unused disallowed interest carried forward to 2022/23 of 10,800 (£13,500 - £2,700).

Income tax due after deductions: £3,140 - £2,700 = £440.

# 21.   Extracting Capital

HMRC's Business Income Manual (BIM45700) confirms that a property owner can remortgage and extract capital from the lettings business so long as the capital account does not become overdrawn.

The Manual gives an example of a landlord acquiring a flat for £125,000 with a mortgage of £80,000. He lets it when it is valued at £375,000 and remortgages so the total debt is £205,000, extracting £125,000 of capital to spend on a private asset. All of the mortgage interest (including the extra payable on the additional loan) will be tax deductible subject to the interest relief restriction rules (see Tip 19).

However, a tax case has put doubt on this section of the Manual and following a First Tribunal Tier tax case of *HMRC v Vowles 2017 TC 06123* HMRC's revised view is that interest payments must be incurred to provide working capital for the business and not be extracted to use for private purposes.

# 22.   Portfolio Mortgages

Tax relief is allowed on interest paid on mortgages/loans taken out to finance the purchase of assets held within a business. Landlords who own two or more properties are deemed to own a 'portfolio' of business assets.

Lenders have designed products that treat the 'portfolio' as one single business account regardless of the number of properties purchased or whether the full amount of capital has been utilised. The individual properties may have separate mortgages each with different interest rates charged but the 'portfolio' is treated as one single business account. 'One portfolio' means one agreement, one monthly payment, and one mortgage statement.

Should not all of the capital be used, tax credit relief on interest payments is still fully allowable (subject to the restrictions given in Tip 19) because the original reason  for the mortgage/loan remains, namely, to finance the use of capital by a property business (assuming that the capital remains in the business for further investment rather than withdrawing for personal use).

If the capital amount exceeds the value of the property when first let the interest on the amount by which it is exceeded is disallowed.

## Portfolio Mortgages

Avril owns six properties with a total current value of £2m (in excess of the original value). With a portfolio mortgage outstanding of £1.7m there is a 'shortfall' of £300,000. This amount is not the equity found in any one property, but in the portfolio spread over the six properties.

Therefore £300,000 is available for further investment.

## 23.  Loan Finance Costs

The costs of obtaining loan finance are tax deductible from income subject to the interest relief restriction for personal landlords of residential property (see Tip 19). Full allowance is claimable for the purchase of non-residential (commercial) properties or residential properties owned by a company or Limited Liability Partnership.

Dependent on the type of loan obtained, the following are allowable in relation to the loan itself:

• Legal and professional expenses for the negotiation of a loan and preparing documents.

• Underwriting commissions, brokerage, and introduction fees.

• Land registry fees, search fees, and valuer's fees in connection with the security of the loan.

• Commitment fees for an undertaking to make the loan available.

• Costs of replacing or varying a loan.

Some lenders add the costs of setting up the loan to the loan itself. Provided these costs are allowable, the interest associated with the relevant part of the loan is also allowable.

A lender usually charges a penalty on the early repayment of the loan. HMRC accepts this as a cost relating to the loan itself and it is, therefore, deductible as an expense against income.

If the expense is deemed not income tax deductible this does not necessarily mean that no relief is available. It may be possible to claim against capital gains tax when the property is eventually sold.

# 24.   Repairs

Work carried out to an existing or newly acquired property that results in the property being improved or altered is deemed to be a capital expense, deductible in the capital gains tax calculation on sale.

If a property is acquired in a derelict or run-down state and the price paid was substantially reduced then expenditure incurred in repairing and putting it in a fit state for letting or use in a business may be capital rather than revenue expenditure.

Repairs such as painting and redecorating, mending broken windows, replacing tiles, etc. are allowable deductions from the rental income.

If a business rents out a commercial property and under the terms of the lease the tenant is required to incur the cost of repairs, then the expense is allowed against the profits of the tenant's business even though the property is now owned by the tenant as the cost is required to enable the tenant's business to continue.

## 25.  'Replacement Furniture' Relief

Under the 'Replacement Furniture' Relief rules landlords of all residential lets (except furnished holiday lets) whether partly furnished or unfurnished, are able to claim a deduction for the capital costs of replacing such items as furniture, furnishings, appliances and kitchenware provided by the landlord for use by the tenant.

No deduction is permitted for the initial cost of the furnishings or to the extent that any replacement expenditure is actually an improvement of enhancement.

A replacement will be regarded as an 'improvement or enhancement' if the item can do more than the item replaced.

### 'Replacement Furniture' Relief

Landlord John spends £600 replacing the existing washing machine with a washer dryer. The cost of an equivalent washing machine to the one replaced is £400.

The permitted deduction would be £400 (the cost of a 'like-for-like' replacement) rather than £600. The additional £200 spent on the washer dryer is regarded as 'improvement' expenditure and is not allowable.

# 26.   Pre-Letting Expenses

Expenses may be incurred in the setting up of a letting business before the first rental receipt is received (travel, phone, advertising, etc.). If so, deduction from rental income may be possible once the letting starts.

Relief is only allowable under these special rules where the expenditure is:

- incurred within a period of seven years before the date the rental business actually starts;

- is not otherwise allowable as a deduction for tax purposes (i.e. against any other income or capital gain);

- would have been allowed as a deduction if it had been incurred after the rental business started.

Letting expenditure incurred pre-commencement is treated as having been incurred on the day on which the rental business starts and added to other allowable letting expenses incurred during the tax year. This total amount is then deducted from the total letting receipts for that year.

The expense must not be for the purchase of capital items. Capital expenditure is potentially tax deductible but there are separate rules of calculation (see Chapter 3 for detail).

Costs incurred in relation to the actual purchase of the property, including legal fees, are a capital cost allowed against the proceeds of the eventual disposal of property under the capital gains tax rules.

The seven year rule is of limited use to a landlord who previously lived in the property as his main residence as it would be hard to argue that the work had been carried out 'wholly and exclusively' for letting.

## 27.  Pre-Letting Repairs

Expenses incurred for the repair and maintenance of items prior to the first letting income received may be allowable provided certain conditions are met, namely that:

- The cost is for the replacement of worn or dilapidated items.

- The property was in a fit state of repair for use in the letting business prior to it actually being let.

- The price paid for the property was not substantially reduced to take into account its dilapidated state of repair.

- The purchase price, if reduced, was reduced only to take into account *'normal wear and tear'*.

### Pre Letting repairs

The surveyor's report undertaken on the purchase of a property will often include an estimate of the rental income that could be derived from a property, which can be useful evidence that the property was in a 'fit state of repair' before money is spent on repairs.

Alternatively, the taking of photographs before repairs are undertaken could be admitted as proof.

# 28.   Post-Letting Expenses

Where there is only one property being let then when the letting contract ceases there will be no income against which relief can be claimed. However, by ensuring that any expense is accrued (allowed) for, tax relief is available. The crucial factor is not when the expense is paid or the date on the invoice but when the need for the expense arose.

If the business comprises a 'portfolio' of properties then any expenses are deductible from rental income from the business as a whole.

## Post-Letting Expenses

Last year Tony rented a property to a couple who left suddenly without giving notice. When Tony entered the property he found it in need of substantial redecoration and repair. A couple of weeks later a reminder for an unpaid electricity bill arrived. What expenses can be claimed?

Damage to property – as the property had been damaged whilst the property was let (or available to let) the expense of repair can be claimed.

Electricity bill – although the bill is not Tony's legal responsibility (as it will be issued in the name of the previous tenant), if he is unable to find the whereabouts of the previous tenants he will have to pay in order for the electricity supply not to be cut off. The expense is a cost of the letting and is therefore allowable.

# 29.    Expenses On Cessation

Where a non-corporate property business ceases (usually when the final property is sold or the property is no longer let) then relief for expenses incurred post cessation may be available for offset against current income. The claim is possible where, within seven years of the business ceasing, the taxpayer is required to make a 'qualifying payment', or a 'qualifying event' has occurred in connection with the ceased business.

'Qualifying payments' include the remedying of defective work and legal expenses in connection with such defects, or expenses incurred in collecting outstanding business debts.

'Qualifying events' arise when debts taken into account in calculating the profits or losses of the business subsequently prove to be bad, or are released, after cessation.

The relief is against other general income initially with any balance against any capital gains accruing in the same year.

## Expenses On Cessation

Dawn sold the last property in her portfolio on 25 August 2015.

In July 2021 she loses a court case for defective services and is obliged to make a compensation payment of £10,000.

Her taxable income for 2021/22 is estimated as being £30,000.

If she makes a claim by 31 January 2023 she can offset the £10,000 against her 2021/22 income and obtain a tax refund.

# 30.    Expenses On Sale

After the decision has been made to sell a rental property, expenses incurred cannot be deducted from the rental income received after that date. Although there is no specific legal requirement for written confirmation of the date of the decision, it would be advisable to make a note.

With a portfolio of properties, expenses such as stationery, petrol, phone bill, etc. are allowable because, even after a particular property has been sold, a business will still be in place receiving income against which such costs may be deducted.

Repair costs incurred on a property that is in the process of being sold are not generally deductible against the letting income. They also cannot be utilised as capital expenditure against the sale proceeds as the cost of maintaining a capital asset is not deductible for capital gains tax purposes.

Most importantly, loan interest accruing after the last tenant has left and the decision has been made to sell cannot be included in a tax reduction relief claim as the property no longer forms part of the letting business. (see Tip 19).

## 31.   Property Let At Less Than Market Rate

HMRC do not have the power to tell a landlord how much to charge as rent but they can restrict the amount of expenses claimed against any rent that is paid.

HMRC take the view that unless the landlord charges the full market rent for a property and imposes normal market lease conditions, it is unlikely that the expenses of the property are incurred *'wholly and exclusively'* in the rental of the property. HMRC will be prepared to allow expenses to be deducted up to the amount of rent received, thereby producing neither a taxable profit nor an allowable loss.

Should there be any excess expenses incurred on properties let at less than the market rent, then the excess cannot be carried forward for deduction against rental income received in a subsequent tax year. Losses incurred on such a property simply do not exist.

Properties let 'rent free' are regarded by HMRC as being tax neutral and outside the scope of the property income tax regime.

To ensure that the property does not lose its 'business' status it needs to remain available for letting even if it is being used 'rent free' for a time. Such a situation may arise if a landlord has allowed tenants to remain 'rent free' in the property whilst at the same time the property is on the market for replacement paying tenants. During the 'Covid 19' pandemic many landlords allowed tenants to live 'rent free' and although not specifically addressed at the time of publication it is hoped that HHMRC will take a lenient view.

Losses incurred on such a property simply do not exist - it is not that the losses cannot be offset (whether against income on the same property or against income from other properties in the rental business), rather that they are not allowed to arise in the first place.

# 32.   'Rent-A-Room' Relief

The 'Rent-A-Room' relief scheme is a tax exemption scheme that allows property owners who let out spare furnished rooms in their only or main home to receive up to £7,500 per annum gross and not be subject to tax. The relief is automatic where the rental income is less than the threshold.

If the rent received exceeds £7,500, the first £7,500 is tax free, income tax being paid on the balance. This obviously covers income from lodgers and may also apply to bed and breakfast or guest houses which would usually be assessed to tax as a trade. The exemption limit of £7,500 is reduced to £3,750 if, during the tax year, someone else receives income from letting from the same property.

The limit is not reduced if the room is let for less than 12 months, or if rented for only one month or just rented out in term time.

The owner and lodger must occupy the property for at least part of the letting period in each tax year of claim. A comparison can be made year on year and the method changed to cater for whichever produces the better result.

## Rent-A-Room Relief

Julie is a higher rate 40% taxpayer who lets out her spare room for a total of £9,000 per year to include the provision of breakfast.

For 2020/21, the taxable amount is calculated as follows:

| | |
|---|---|
| Gross income | £ 9,000 |
| Relief | £(7,500) |
| Balance to be taxed | £ 1,500 |

Tax payable at the 40% rate = £60.

In the subsequent year 2021/22, Julie estimates that although she will receive the same gross amount of £9,000, she will incur costs of £10,000, producing a loss of £(1,000).

For this year it would be more beneficial to prepare normal property income and expense accounts claiming the loss of £(1,000), rather than claiming 'Rent-A-Room' relief.

The loss can generally be claimed against other property income – or carried forward and offset against future net profits.

# 33.   Property Allowance

The Property Allowance provides for full tax relief if an individual's property income for the year is less than £1,000. If this is the case and the landlord has no other income subject to self-assessment then there is no requirement to file a tax return. Where the landlord makes over £1,000 in rental income they must let HMRC know that they have a source of rental income. This needs to be done by 5 October after the tax year in which the income arises.

Landlords who qualify for full relief in one year will need to monitor their property income year on year as if it goes above £1,000 they will be required to register and submit returns.

A partial relief claim is available where the property income exceeds £1,000. Under this claim a landlord can choose either to:

• Deduct actual property business expenses from the income in the usual way; or

• Elect instead for the £1,000 property allowance to be given as a deduction from income.

A 'rent-a-room' property business does not qualify for this allowance nor is it available should the landlord qualify for 'rent-a-room' relief but chooses not to make a claim (see Tip 32). Therefore, the property allowance is most likely to be of benefit for commercial property lettings or holiday homes with minimal expenses.

If when a landlord prepares his annual accounts he/she finds that a loss has been made rather than a projected profit then if an election is not made to disapply the Allowance then these losses cannot be claimed. The election can be made at any time up to 31 January 2023 for the 2021/22 tax year.

# 34.    Furnished Holiday Lettings

The operation of a furnished holiday let (FHL) is deemed to be a business and not a property income investment. As such the usual business income and expenditure accounts are prepared and expenses claimed. This treatment creates a number of benefits for the personal landlord:

- Pension contributions can be deducted from profit.

- Capital gains tax reliefs available - Rollover relief, Gift relief (see Tip 77), Business Asset Disposal Relief (see Tip 58).

- Capital Allowances can be claimed (see Chapter 3).

- Losses are carried forward unless part of the loss arises from a capital allowance claim.

**Conditions:**

- Accommodation must be 'available' for short-term letting for 210 days in any one tax year and actually be let for 105 days of the year.

- Accommodation should not normally be in the same property for a continuous period of 31 days in a period of 155 days in any one tax year. Long-term letting should not exceed 155 days ('occupation' condition).

The 'occupation' test can be met by making an election to 'average out' periods of occupation of any or all of the FHLs owned. This test is satisfied if all of the FHL properties in total are let for 105 days in the tax year on average. The election needs to be made separately for properties in the UK and EEA.

Rent must be charged at a market rate. The rental profit or losses are kept separate from other non- FHL property, such that losses can only be offset against income of the same FHL business. 'Replacement Furniture Relief' (see Tip 25) does not apply.

**'Period of Grace' election**

Should the landlord have only one FHL property that does not satisfy the 'occupancy' condition in any one year or he/she is unable to claim under the 'Averaging' election because the actual occupation days were too low then the 'period of grace' election should be considered.

This election is used where the landlord intended to meet the 'occupancy' condition but for whatever reason was unable to do so. The pattern of 'occupation' and 'availability' conditions must still be met but should the property qualify for FHL in one accounting period or tax year out of every three but does not qualify in the next or next two years then the election treats the year that does not qualify to be included in the calculation. This means that should the FHL qualifying conditions be achieved in 2020/21 for example, FHL status in 2020/21 and 2021/22 will be possible even if the 'occupancy' condition is not met in either of those years.

Unfortunately, the election does not extend to a new FHL business as the qualifying criteria must be met throughout the 365-day period from the first commercial letting of the property. Importantly, the 365 days do not need to cover the tax year.

If the conditions are not satisfied then the property will be taxed under the normal rental rules, not being treated as a trading activity for tax purposes rather than the more beneficial FHL rules. This will mean that the landlord will not being able to benefit from pension contribution reliefs (apart from the £3,600 net of tax relief permitted to all taxpayers), certain capital gains tax reliefs or be able to claim capital allowances for such items as furniture, fixtures and equipment.

# Chapter 3.
# Capital Allowances

# 35.  Annual Investment Allowance

Capital allowances are available on the purchase of certain fixed asset items used in a letting business. Landlords who let residential property cannot generally claim capital allowances and as such they are more likely to be claimed by landlords of commercial property as 'plant and machinery'. The claim encompasses assets such as lifts, central heating and air-conditioning. Furnished holiday lettings are deemed to be a 'trade' and, therefore capital allowances can be claimed.

Capital allowances cannot be claimed if the default 'cash basis' for calculation is used, claims only being possible under the 'accrual' basis of calculation (see Tip 14).

The Annual Investment Allowance (AIA) is a 100% allowance on the cost of investment in standard plant and machinery subject to a 'permanent' limit amount of £200,000. There has been a temporary increase of the allowance to £1 million for the two years from 1 January 2019 to 31 December 2021 which will revert back to the £200,000 limit after 1 January 2022. The limits are proportionately reduced where the accounting period is less than 12 months.

However, the temporary rules have imposed a 'cap' on the amount of expenditure incurred in that part of the accounting period falling on or after 1 January 2021.

The cap is found by applying the formula:

y/12 x £200,000

where y is the number of days in the accounting period after 31 December 2021.

Therefore the maximum AIA available to a company with a 12-month tax period from 1 April 2021 to 31 March 2022 would be £802,740, calculated as follows:

1.  1 April to 31 December 2021:

    £1,000,000 x 275/365 days = £753,425 and

2.  1 January to 31 March 2022: £200,000 x 90/365 days = £49,315

Any balance of allowances not used under AIA is transferred into the Writing Down Pool.

# 36.  Excess Expenditure

Where the Annual Investment Allowance (AIA) is not claimed or not available because the limit (or 'cap' under the transitional rules - see Tip 35) has already been reached, tax relief is given on the purchase of capital items on a reducing balance termed the 'writing down allowance'.

Expenditure in excess of the AIA limit enters either the main pool or a 'special rate' pool for the purchase of integrated features (see Tip 38) and is eligible for the writing down allowance at 18% per annum (main pool) or 6% ('special rate' pool) in the accounting period.

Should any of the pooled assets be sold, the proceeds are deducted from the pool amount brought forward thereby reducing the value against which further writing down allowances can be claimed.

## Excess Expenditure

Company ASX Ltd has an accounting year ending 30 June. The pool balance brought forward as at 1 July 2020 was £53,300. On 3 January 2021 the company invested £650,000 in refurbishing a substantial block of furnished holiday lets - replacing kitchen, bathrooms and security systems. No further assets were purchased.

| | |
|---|---|
| Pool balance brought forward 01.07.2020 | £ 53,300 |
| Additions qualifying for AIA 2020/21 | £650,000 |
| AIA claim maximum ** | £600,000 |
| Balance allocated to main pool | £ 50,000 |

| | |
|---|---|
| Total eligible for writing down allowance | £ 103,300 |
| Writing down allowance (18%) 2019/20 | £( 18,594) |
| Balance of allowances carried forward | £ 84,706 |
| Writing Down Allowance (18%) 2020/21 | £(15,247) |
| Balance of allowances carried forward | £69,279 |

Total allowances claimed 2020/21: £600,000 + £15,247 = £615,427.

** Maximum: (£200,000 x 6/12) + (£1 million (temporary 'uplift') x 6/12).

# 37.   Restricted Claim

Capital allowances available on assets purchased for use in a property business need not be claimed in full; the amount can be restricted by choice if it is more tax efficient to do so. For example this would be relevant to reduce the profit to the personal allowance such that no tax is payable and the maximum amount of allowances is preserved to be carried forward for future years.

| Restricted Claim |
| --- |
| Jane's property business has a main pool written down value brought forward of £80,000. Profit for the year to 5 April 2021 is £19,000; she has no other income. |

The personal allowance for 2021/22 is £12,570.

Note: In this example restricting the claim to £6,500 reduces the net profit down to exactly the personal allowance so no tax is due. The balance of allowances of £7,900 remains in the 'pool' for carry forward.

| | |
| --- | --- |
| Pool balance brought forward | £80,000 |
| Max writing down allowance possible at 18% | £14,400 |
| Amount of actual claim (restricted) | £(6,430) |
| Balance added to 'pool' | £ 7,970 |
| Balance to carry forward | **£73,570** |

**Tax calculation:**

| | |
| --- | --- |
| Profit | £19,000 |
| Less writing down allowance claim | £(6,430) |
| Net profit | £ 12,570 |
| Personal Allowance 2020/21 | £(12,570) |
| | |
| Tax liability | NIL |

## 38.   'Special Rate' 'Integral Features Allowance

Expenditure on 'integral features' for non-residential buildings or furnished holiday letting come under the capital allowances rules as expenditure on plant and machinery. In line with other forms of plant and machinery, relief is given by means of either an Annual Investment Allowance (AIA) or a writing down allowance claim - however, special rules apply.

'Integral features' include:

• solar heating;

• electrical system, including a lighting system;

• cold water system;

• heating system, a powered system of ventilation, air cooling or air purification, and any floor or ceiling in such a system;

• lift or escalator.

Any item not on this list (even if forming part of the building) is outside the scope of the integral features' rules.

Expenditure on such assets in excess of any claim under the AIA is allocated to a 'special rate' pool and 6% written down allowance can be claimed.

Special rules also apply to expenditure on the replacement of such items as well as to the provision.

## 'Special Rate' Integral Features Allowance

James needs to replace the electrical system in his factory at a total cost of £200,000.

He pays a 40% deposit of £80,000 on 30 December 2021 before the end of his 31 December 2021 accounting year with the balance being paid on 30 June 2022 once the work has been completed.

Although the deposit falls within the 2020 accounting period and would normally attract 100% AIA, as the deposit represented only 40% of the replacement cost, that deposit plus the final payment was incurred within the same 12 months. As that total represented more than 50% of the replacement cost, the total expenditure of £200,000 is deemed to be capital expenditure and allocated to the 'special rate' pool, attracting WDAs at 6%.

Usually an item being replaced is treated as an income tax deduction under the 'Replacement furniture' relief rules (see Tip 25). However, where it is an integral feature that is being replaced then should that cost exceed 50% of the original item then the expenditure is not deductible against income, rather it is capitalised and subject to capital allowances.

To calculate the 50% the rules look back over a period of 12 months beginning with the date that the initial expenditure was incurred in case payment was split and paid in instalments.

# 39. Cars

If a van is used in the letting business to travel between properties or from office to property, the purchase cost is allowable in full so long as the cash basis of calculation is used. Otherwise a claim under the Annual Investment Allowance (AIA) capital allowances rules is possible if the 'accrual' basis of calculation is used (see Tip 14).

AIA cannot be claimed on the purchase of cars as, although the purchase comes under the capital allowances regime, the claim has to be as a writing down allowance (WDA) of 18% per annum (or 6% if the vehicle's CO2 emissions exceed 110g/km). The allowance is 100% if a new car with CO2 of 50g/km.

The claim can only represent the proportion of business use of the asset – private use being disallowed. It is difficult to claim the full WDA successfully on a car owned by an unincorporated landlord because HMRC will normally argue that the car must be used privately to some extent. However, if the car is owned by a company and is required to be garaged on company premises overnight with private use essentially being forbidden, then the whole WDA can be deducted from the company's profits.

It should be noted that if a claim is made under the 'simplified expenses' rules then capital allowances cannot be claimed (see Tip 17).

## Cars

David purchased a car for use in his letting business – the car's value is £5,000 with CO2 emissions of 165g/km. He calculates that the car is used 75% of the time on business.

The WDA claim for 2021/22 will be calculated as:

£5,000 x 6% x 75% =£225.

The amount carried forward to 2022/23= £4,600 (i.e. £5,000 – £300 being the total WDA before restricting for private use).

# 40.  Ancillary Expenses

When a property business undertakes expenditure that is capital in nature such that a capital allowance is claimed, then that cost can be augmented by 'ancillary' expenses.

Such ancillary expenses include labour and material expenses paid to install an item of plant or equipment plus costs of structural alterations to a building to accommodate the new plant.

Professional fees paid to architects or structural engineers can also be claimed provided it can be proved that the costs relate directly to the installation of the plant and machinery.

## Ancillary Expenses

The availability of tax relief on ancillary expenses produces a tax planning possibility.

Tony bought a commercial building but after an inspection was advised to install a lift. A lift is eligible for capital allowances, but the actual lift shaft is considered to be part of the building.

If the lift had been installed at the time of building, the cost of the lift shaft would be ineligible for capital allowances and as such would not be relievable until the sale of the building as a capital gains tax cost.

However, as Tony has decided to install the lift after the building has been built the lift shaft becomes ancillary to the installation of qualifying machinery, is an ancillary cost and as such is allowable for capital allowances.

# 41.   Sale Of Commercial Property (1)

When a commercial property is sold, part of the selling price will include the value of fixtures that have qualified for capital allowances in the seller's business.

If the proceeds of sale on those assets exceed the written down value of the 'pool' there will be a 'balancing charge'. A 'balancing charge' is treated as a negative allowance whereby any capital allowances previously claimed will be clawed back.

It is mandatory for a formal 's198 election' to be made between the two parties, enabling agreement of a value for capital allowances purposes only, not exceeding the original purchase price of the assets. If the parties do not agree to this joint election, the purchaser (and any subsequent buyer) is prohibited from claiming any capital allowances on those fixtures.

The seller will want to set a value as low as possible to maximise allowances, but the purchaser will want to agree a value that enables him or her to make some amount of claim carrying forward.

## Sale Of Commercial Property (1)

In 2021 Steve sells an industrial unit to Fred for an agreed price of £300,000.

Steve originally purchased the unit in 2007 for £250,000 and has previously claimed capital allowances on air conditioning and security systems costing £50,000.

If the written down value of the assets at the point of Steve's sale to Fred was £20,000 and with the corresponding proceeds value restricted to Steve's original cost of £50,000, £30,000 allowances that

Steve has previously claimed will be 'clawed' back.

If the value agreed under the election is £100, Steve will be able to claim a balancing allowance on sale of £19,900 but Fred will only be able to claim £100 going forward.

# 42.  Sale Of Commercial Property (2)

The tax rules state that the purchaser's entitlement to capital allowances in relation to commercial property is restricted to the disposal value that the vendor of the property brought into account, even if this was not the immediate past owner.

Furthermore, it is the purchaser's responsibility to obtain and provide details of prior claims and disposal values, which might prove difficult if the original owner has ceased trading or if records are no longer available.

It is also a condition that the vendor must 'pool' the qualifying expenditure (i.e. add it to his or her own capital allowances computations). This would include expenditure incurred possibly many years before, which he or she may have neglected to claim previously.

There are some categories of expenditure that the vendor may not have been able to claim at the time the costs were incurred – these may pass through to the purchaser without having been pooled, or be included in a joint 's198 election'. The most likely category is integral features installed before April 2008.

Under a 's198 election' the purchaser and vendor negotiate and elect jointly to set a figure to be treated by both parties as the disposal sale proceeds and purchase price for the fixtures (but not chattels). This figure would also be binding on HMRC and any subsequent purchaser of the property.

## Sale Of Commercial Property (2)

In the tax case of *Mr and Mrs Tapsell and Mr Lester v HMRC (2011) UKFTT 376 TC* the partners purchased a care home as a going concern.

They made a claim for capital allowances totalling £146,014 – the figure being based on an apportionment of the purchase price.

£106,014 of this amount related to the purchase of plant and machinery plus £40,000 that had been allocated as 'fixtures and fittings' in the contract.

Shortly afterwards, the sellers submitted a capital allowances claim of £68,811 for the same tax year. They provided no supporting details to HMRC, they then emigrated and could not be traced by either Mr and Mrs Tapsell or HMRC.

HMRC disallowed Mr and Mrs Tapsell's capital allowances claim on the grounds that they failed to show that the sellers had not previously claimed allowances on those fixtures.

# Chapter 4.
# Losses

# 43.  General

Losses on a property business are calculated in the same way as losses on a trading business.

Separate 'pools' are used for similar types of property, e.g. those not let on a commercial basis and foreign properties. Therefore, two distinct and separate 'pools' will be created should there be both UK and foreign properties in a portfolio (see Tip 1).

Losses made on the same type of property are automatically offset against profits made on other properties in the same portfolio for the same period – being 'pooled' together.

Losses on furnished holiday lettings (FHLs) are kept separate and cannot be offset against either other UK rental profits or profits made on foreign properties.

## General

Joan owns two properties – one in France and one in London.

She lets out both properties – the London one for the full year but the one in France for only two months over the summer. She makes a net profit on the property in London but a net loss on the one in France. Neither constitutes an FHL. The loss on the French property cannot be offset against the profits made on the London property and must be kept separate.

However, the loss can be carried forward and deducted against any profit made on any future lettings of the French property or indeed, on any other overseas non-FHL properties Joan might subsequently acquire.

# 44.  Loss relief

If there is an overall income tax loss made for a tax year, then unless the loss arises in relation to certain capital allowances, the loss is generally relieved as follows:

- Carried forward and set against profits made in future years on properties in the same UK property business (or if overseas property, against the same overseas property business).

- If the loss arises on or after cessation, relief may be set against the owners' general income or against capital gains made, in certain circumstances.

- Any losses brought forward can only be carried forward and relieved against profits of the same property business. This means that if one property business ceases and few years later a new rental business starts, the losses from the old business cannot be set against any profits from the new business, as the two businesses are not the same.

- Losses from UK furnished holiday lettings (FHLs) can only be carried forward and set against profits made on other UK FHL properties. When a property ceases to be an FHL, any unclaimed losses are wasted. Should the property be continued to be let, but as unfurnished, then the income and expenditure will be pooled with any other non-furnished lettings and taxed accordingly. For further detail on FHL see Tip 34.

- For investment in overseas property, the rules are modified so that losses are automatically carried forward to subsequent accounting periods. It is not possible to set-off against total profits, as is the case with a UK property business.

# 45.   Excess Capital Allowances

Although the general rule is that losses from a property rental business can only be relieved by carry forward and offers against future profits of the same property business, there is a limited set off available for commercial properties. If there is an overall income tax loss on an individual's continuing commercial property portfolio over a tax year and that loss has been created by excess capital allowances claimed, then the loss can be relieved by being offset against the owner's other ('general') income for the same and/or next tax year. Otherwise the loss is automatically carried forward and set against future profits of the same UK property business.

The loss would best be used against other income for the same and/or next tax year if the taxpayer had taxable income in excess of the personal allowance.

If other income exceed the personal allowance, better tax planning would be to carry forward the loss, so as not to waste the loss against income already covered by the personal allowance; capital allowances can be disclaimed (restricted) to suit (if the properties are commercial of Furnished Holiday Lets).

The loss can be set against the current year, or the following year, or both if large enough. An unutilised loss is carried forward for offset against future rental profits.

Where a taxpayer makes a loss in his or her UK or overseas property business and the loss has either a capital allowances connection or a relevant agricultural connection, an amount (known as the applicable amount of the loss) can be deducted in calculating a person's net income for the tax year in which the loss was made or the following tax year.

## Excess Capital Allowances

James owns a portfolio of four non residential properties. He purchased a van for use in the letting business claiming full Annual Investment Allowance (AIA- see Tip 35) - this resulted in an overall loss of £10,000.

If he is a taxpayer with income in excess of the personal allowance he can claim for the loss to be offset, thereby reducing his taxable income resulting in a possible tax refund.

If he has no other income the loss should be carried forward and offset against profits of the future period, if any.

He cannot restrict the loss relief claim to the personal allowance as the claim must be for amount, even if this means that the personal allowance is 'wasted'. However, he could restrict the AIA claim to reduce any profit down to the personal allowance. Any excess over the AIA aim is then added to the writing down allowance 'pool' for next year.

# 46.  Loss Relief 'Cap'

Taxpayers seeking to obtain in excess of £50,000 of otherwise unlimited income tax reliefs in any one year are restricted in their claim to the higher of:

- 25% of their total income, or

- £50,000.

One of the tax reliefs relevant to this restriction is property tax loss relief available for offset against total income – most commonly this will apply where some or all of the loss is attributable to capital allowances. The limit does not apply to carry-forward loss relief for a property business under the 'cash' basis of assessment (see Tip 14).

The 'capped' loss will not be wasted as it can be relieved by offset against the owner's other ('general') income in the next tax year, with any 'uncapped' amount being carried forward and set against future profits of the same UK property business.

## Loss Relief 'Cap'

Mark has estimated total income for 2021/22 of £300,000. He makes pension contributions of £30,000 gross, is estimated to pay £50,000 in (non-property related) loan interest and will have a property loss eligible for sideways relief of £30,000.

The amount of 'uncapped reliefs' equals £80,000, exceeding the 'cap' 'de minimus' of £50,000. The total 'uncapped' relief thus available for offset is calculated as (£300,000 – £30,000 pension) x 25% = £67,500.

It would be preferable for the loan interest to be claimed in full together with £17,500 of the property loss, the remainder being carried forward and available for offset against the 2022/23 total income.

# 47.  Dormant Periods

Losses from a residential rental business can only be set against future profits if the business is a continuing business.

In some instances, it will not be clear as to whether a rental business has ceased as the activities may stop and then restart. The losses of a ceased rental business cannot be set against the profits of a 'new' rental business.

HMRC apply a general ruling by which they regard the 'old' rental business as ceasing if there is a gap of at least three years between lets and different properties are let in the taxpayer's old and new letting activities.

A rental business is not normally treated as having ceased simply because the property is not let for a period to allow for repairs or renovations. Other factors include whether the same property was let before and after the dormant period. Therefore a business that had to stop trading due to the Covid 19 'lockdown' but fully intends to recommence trading once the restrictions are lifted, will not be treated as ceasing, so long as, when activities resume, they are the same as before the break. However, the business may be treated as having ceased and then recommencing should the property be used as the taxpayer's main residence between lets.

It is only when a rental business starts carrying out an entirely new type of rental business (e.g. a furnished holiday let) that the question could arise as to whether there has been the commencement of a separate trade.

A Furnished Holiday Let business will cease if the occupancy conditions are not complied with (see Tip 34).

# 48. Capital Losses – Negligible Value

Tax relief is available when an asset is lost, destroyed or becomes of negligible value, e.g. when a 'Buy To Let' property is purchased 'off plan', the builder goes into liquidation, money is lost, and the property is never built.

However, it should be noted that it can be difficult to prove that an asset has *'become'* of negligible value. For example in the tax case of David Harper v CRC [2009] UKFTT 382 the tribunal concurred with HMRC's refusal to allow a negligible value and loss relief claims on shares, contending that the shares were of negligible value at the date of acquisition and so did not *'become'* of negligible value.

To claim the relief:

- The investor must still own the property when it becomes of negligible value.

- The amount of relief is calculated as if the property had been sold and immediately reacquired.

- The claim can be made for an earlier period in the previous two tax years in which the deemed disposal occurred (see example) or for companies, any accounting period ending not more than two years before the date of the claim. This allows the claim to be backdated to a year when the loss can be most profitably used. For the claim to be allowed it may be necessary to demonstrate to HMRC that the asset had already become of negligible value, at that earlier time.

- The claim is not automatic and needs to be made on the Tax Return.

## Capital Losses – Negligible Value

In November 2019 Fred entered into an agreement with a developer to buy two flats 'off plan' for £200,000 each. A deposit of 10% was paid plus legal fees of £3,500.

In July 2020 Fred received a letter informing him that the developer had gone into liquidation.

A year later, in July 2021, it is confirmed that the development will not be going ahead and therefore Fred will not be receiving repayment of the deposit.

Calculation: ((£200,000 x 2 x 10%) + £3,500).

The loss of £(43,500) is treated as a normal capital loss for either offset against other capital gains made during the same year of claim or carried forward against future gains.

The offset could have been applied in the 2020/21 tax year on the basis that this was the year in which the money was 'lost'.

# 49.   Capital Losses – Negligible Value – Planning

Tax planning possibility:

- Disposals between spouses/civil partners are deemed to occur on a 'no gain/no loss' basis.

- If one spouse/civil partner own an asset which, on sale, has produced a capital gain in excess of the annual exempt amount and the other spouse/civil partner has an asset standing at a potential negligible-value loss, the negligible value asset can be transferred to the spouse/civil partner, the loss offset, and capital gain reduced.

---

### Capital Losses – Negligible Value – Planning

Continued from Tip 48 example.

As at 1 July 2021 the flats stand at a negligible-value loss of £(43,500).

In August 2021 Fred's wife sells a separate property owned in her own name producing a chargeable capital gain of £60,000.

If Fred were to transfer the loss-making asset to his wife by 5 April 2022, the end of the tax year, she could offset the loss against the gains made and receive a reduced capital gains tax bill.

# Chapter 5.
# Foreign Matters

# 50.  Non-Resident Landlord Scheme

The 'Non-Resident Landlord Scheme' (NRLS) is a scheme for taxing the UK rental income of non-resident landlords. Usually basic rate tax is deducted from the net rent collected by an agent (less expenses paid) unless the agent/tenant has authority from HMRC to pay the landlord gross. If there is no agent then the tax is supposed to be deducted by the tenant and they pay over to HMRC (see Tip 52).

'Non-resident landlords' under this scheme are persons (individuals, companies, trustees) who are in receipt of UK rental income, and whose 'usual place of abode' is outside of the UK.

Although the scheme refers to 'non-resident' landlords, it is the 'usual place of abode' and not residency that determines whether a landlord is within the scheme or not.

An absence from the UK of six months or more determines that a person has a 'usual place of abode' outside of the UK. It is therefore possible for a person to be tax resident in the UK yet, for the purposes of the scheme, to have a 'usual place of abode' outside of the UK.

Rent can be paid gross on application using Form NRL1. HMRC will formally approve the application where they are satisfied that the applicant's UK tax affairs are up-to-date or that the rental income will be non-taxable (e.g. where covered by personal allowances) or where the applicant does not expect to be liable to UK tax for the tax year for which application is made.

On receipt of the 'Notice of Approval' tax is not to be withheld and a tenant will not be required to make any returns post the date of approval. An agent will have to submit an annual return but will not be required to submit the usual quarterly returns (see next Tip).

# 51.  NRLS – Agents

The 'Non-Resident Landlord Scheme' (NRLS) requires persons who act as 'representatives' (agents) for the landlord to deduct basic rate tax from the net rent collected (rental income less expenses paid) unless the agent or tenant has authority from HMRC to pay the landlord gross (see previous Tip).

The tax is paid on a quarterly basis and an information return is submitted. Payment must be within 30 days of the end of the quarter.

An annual return Form NRLY must be submitted by 5 July after each tax year-end and a certificate issued to the landlord confirming tax paid by the same date.

The quarters are to 30 June, 30 September, 31 December and 31 March.

## NRLS – Agents

John has been working abroad for eight months and rents out his UK property via a letting agent. The letting agent pays all expenses on his behalf, deducting them from the rent received.

The property is let at £800 per month with expenses of £250. The total net rent collected is calculated as being:

£(800 – 250) x 8 months = £4,400.

The tax bill is £110 per month - ((£4,400 /8) @ 20%)).

The amount that John receives per month is £800 – £250 – £110 =

£440.

# 52.   NRLS – Non-Agent

The 'Non-Resident Landlords Scheme' (NRLS) requires that should there be no UK-based representative/agent and the rent is paid directly to a landlord who lives outside of the UK, then that tenant is supposed to deduct basic rate tax from the rent paid and pay over to HMRC.

- The calculation is of tax on the gross amount actually payable to the landlord (plus any payments made by the tenant where the payment is not a deductible expense).

- Tenants do not have to operate the scheme if the rent paid is less than £5,200 per annum.

- Where the tenant occupies the property for only part of the year the threshold of £5,200 is proportionately reduced.

- Where two or more people share a property as tenants the £5,200 limit applies separately to each in respect of each share of the rent.

- The tenant must register with HMRC, make the tax payment plus submit an information return to HMRC confirming tax paid on a quarterly basis within 30 days of the end of each quarter (30 June, 30 September, 31 December and 31 March).

- By 5 July after the tax year-end, the tenant must submit an annual return to HMRC and a certificate to the landlord confirming payments made.

Further details of the scheme can be found at: https://www.gov.uk/tax-uk-income-live-abroad/rent.

# 53.   NRLS – Excess Expenses

Under the 'Non-Resident Landlord Scheme' (NRLS) where the deductible expenses exceed rental income for any quarter the excess expenses are:

- carried back for offset against rental income paid to the same landlord for previous quarters in the same tax year, on a 'last in, first out' basis; then

- carried forward for offset against future quarters' net rental profits.

Carry back will result in a repayment of tax for the previous quarter in the tax year – the amount can be deducted from any tax due for other NRLS lettings of the current quarter.

Should it not be possible to deduct the refund because it relates to a previous tax year, a claim to HMRC is required.

| NRLS – Excess Expenses |
|---|
| John has been working abroad for nine months and rents out his UK property via a letting agent. The letting agent pays all the expenses on his behalf, deducting them from the rent received. |

The property is let at £800 per quarter. There were expenses for the quarter to 31 December 2020 of £200, for the quarter to 31 March 2021 were £1,000, £1,400 for the quarter to 30 June 2021 were £1,400.

Tax year 2020/21

Quarter to 31 December 2020

| | |
|---|---|
| Rent | £800 |
| Less expenses | £(200) |

| Profit | £600 |
|---|---|
| Tax | 120 |

**Quarter to 31 March 2021**

| Rent | £800 |
|---|---|
| Less expenses | £(1,000) |
| Carry back loss to previous quarter | £(200) |
| Tax refund £200 @ 20% | £40 |

**Tax year 2021/22**

**Quarter to 30 June 2021**

| Rent | £800 |
|---|---|
| Less expenses | £(1,400) |
| Excess expenses | £(600) |

The £(600) excess cannot be carried back to the previous quarter, as the quarter is not in the same tax year. Rather, it will be carried forward to be offset against future net profit (if the property remains rented). If the property ceases to be rented the excess cannot be used by the agent.

# Chapter 6.
# Selling Property

# 54.   Capital Gains Tax

Capital gains tax (CGT) is charged on the net gains (proceeds less cost) made on the sale of assets by individuals, personal representatives and trustees. Companies do not pay CGT, rather they are charged to corporation tax on net gains made.

### Charge to CGT

A UK resident and domiciled property investor is liable to CGT where:

- a property is sold at a higher price than the original purchase price wherever situated in the world, or

- a property or part of a property is transferred to an individual who is not the transferor's spouse/civil partner.

UK resident but non-domiciled persons are liable to CGT on UK assets and on gains brought into the country (known as the 'remittance basis').

A non UK resident is liable to CGT on the disposal of UK property or land, of mixed use UK property or land, or rights to assets that derive at least 75% of their value from UK land (indirect disposals).

### Calculation

Gains (or losses) are calculated separately for each asset.

- The net gains/losses for each property sold in a tax year are totalled and if the overall gain exceeds the annual exempt amount (£12,300 for individuals in 2021/22), the balance is taxed at the taxpayer's highest rate of tax applicable to capital gains (i.e. for residential property owned by individuals the rate is 18% for any amount falling within the basic rate band and 28% for the higher rate bands).

- A disposal may give rise to a gain or loss.

Other non residential property gains are taxed at 10% if within the basic rate band and 20% otherwise - companies pay CGT at an effective rate of 19%.

The most common and valuable exemption from the charge for individuals is the main Principal Private Residence (PPR) exemption (see Chapter 7)

CGT chargeable on the sale of any property not covered by Principal Private residence must be declared and paid to HMRC within 30 days of sale (see next Tip 55).

# 55.   Declaration And Payment Of CGT

Any taxpayer having made a chargeable gain on the disposal of rental property or of any property where the gain is not covered by Principal Private Residence relief has 30 calendar days from the date of completion to advice HMRC and to pay the CGT owed, if any (see Chapter 7).

Interest will always be charged if any CGT remains unpaid after the 30 days deadline.

The declaration is via an online Property return separate and in addition to the annual self assessment return and HMRC are able to enquire into it separately. Where the individual is also within self-assessment, it is necessary to report the disposal twice - once within 30 days and then again on the relevant self-assessment return. CGT computations for disposals in 2020/21 will not be pre-populated into self-assessment returns but this is something that HMRC are looking into for future returns.

In a few cases it may be possible for the individual to report the gain just once, via their self-assessment return. In such cases the obligation to file a property return is avoided because the individual is able to file their self-assessment return *before* the 30 day deadline for the Property return.

For example, if the exchange occurred on 2 February 2021, so that the disposal was in the tax year 2020/21, but completion was on 31 May 2021, the individual would have until 30 June 2021 to report for sale. If the 2020/21 self-assessment return was submitted before 30 June 2021 (the tax return must include details of the property disposal), then this removes the obligation to complete a Property return as well. It appears that this will then mean that the original 31 January deadline would apply for any CGT due but this has still to be confirmed with HMRC.

If no gain has been made then no return is required should the taxpayer be UK resident. Non UK residents are required to submit a return 30 days after the disposal even if no liability arises.

## 56.  Consideration – 'Arm's Length' Rule

A property deal is termed as being made at 'arm's length' if it is a normal commercial transaction between two or more persons. A transaction not likely to be at arm's length is one undertaken by persons related by blood, adoption or marriage, or who are living together.

HMRC requires a valuation of property if the transaction has not been made at 'arm's length'. The valuation will determine the market value and that is the figure that will be used as the proceeds amount in the CGT calculation on sale or another disposal.

### Consideration – 'Arm's Length' Rule

Anton needs to sell his property quickly so that he can move abroad. Tony is aware that Anton needs a quick sale and therefore offers him a low price. No one else has made an offer. Anton accepts the offer.

The price was not the best possible price that could have achieved if the property had been left on the market for longer but Anton was trying to achieve the best deal possible in the time allowed.

This is deemed to be a bad bargain rather than being a bargain not made at 'arm's length' and therefore the proceeds received will be used in any CGT calculation.

If Anton and Tony had been related (i.e. 'connected persons') HMRC would require a market valuation.

# 57.  Lettings Relief

Despite its title, 'Lettings Relief' is not available on any property which has been let out but never occupied by the owner as his or her main residence.

The relief is only available for periods of letting where the owner occupied the property with the tenant (e.g. where a person lets out a room or rooms in his main residence and continues to occupy the premises). However, if the owner shares occupancy with a tenant and the owner moves out, lettings relief will not be available for the period after the owner has moved out.

The conditions for the claim are that:

- part of the property is the individual's only or main residence; and
- another part of that property is let out by the individual, otherwise than in the course of a trade or a business.

The gain pertaining to the let part is only chargeable to CGT to the extent that it exceeds the lesser of:

- the amount of the Principal Private Relief; and
- £40,000.

Where a lodger lives as a member of the family, sharing the family's living accommodation and taking meals with them, HMRC takes the view that no part of the accommodation has ceased to be the owner's main residence and as such PPR relief will apply.

However, if the lodger does not live as a member of the family, PPR relief is not available in respect of that part of the property occupied by the lodger and lettings relief should be considered.

## Lettings relief

Amelia has owned a three-bedroom property as her main residence for three years. She rents out one room furnished for £400 per month. The let accommodation comprises 1/6th of the property by floor area.

On selling the property, she realises a gain of £70,000.

The annual rent from letting a room is £4,800. As this is less than the rent-a-room threshold of £7,500, the relief applies automatically and the rental income is therefore free of income tax (see Tip 32).

For CGT purposes the part of the property that is let and not occupied by Amelia as her main residence is not eligible for PPR relief. However, the remaining part is eligible. Therefore PPR relief will apply to the gain arising in the last nine months of ownership of the 1/6th share of the gain and also nine months on 5/6th of the gain attributable to the rental area – a total of 16.5 months.

The property was owned for 36 months and therefore the gain available for PPR relief is £33,083 (i.e. 16.5/36 x £70,000.

The remaining gain of £36,917 is attributable to the letting.

The gain will be tax-free as lettings relief of £40,000 is available to cover the gain relating to the 5/6th let area and PPR is available to cover the gain on the remaining 1/6th area.

# 58.   Business Asset Disposal Relief

Business Asset Disposal Relief (BATR - formerly Entrepreneurs' Relief) is only available on a capital gain arising on the disposal of a business asset that is linked to or takes place as part of, a disposal of all or part of a business. For these purposes, a 'business' is a trade, profession or vocation.

Therefore, the relief is not generally available on disposals of residential property held as an investment but is allowed on the sale of furnished holiday lets (as these properties are regarded as business assets) or commercial property.

Relief is also potentially available on the disposal of a property that has been used as a main residence and a business, in which case the property should be sold no later than nine months after the sale of the business to ensure that the principal private residence relief can be claimed (see Chapter 7 for detail on PPR).

BATR can only be claimed by individuals and not by companies. The effect is to reduce the CGT rate charge from 28% (if the seller landlord is a higher rate taxpayer) or 18% (if the landlord is a basic rate taxpayer) to 10% for residential properties; 20% to 10% for non-residential properties whichever the marginal rate. There is also a lifetime limit of £1m.

The relief extends to disposals made within 36 months of cessation of trading, provided that the business qualified for the two years up to the cessation of the business.

## Business Asset Disposal Relief

Ahmed is a dentist, who runs his practice from a surgery attached to his home, which is calculated as 25% of the property area. He is a basic rate taxpayer.

He is disposing of his home and business on retirement.

The gain on the property disposal is £800,000 and the goodwill is

£400,000.

The tax liability for 2021/22 will be:

| | |
|---|---|
| Gain on home 25% x £800,000 | £200,000 |
| Gain on Goodwill | £400,000 |
| Total Gain | £600,000 |
| Less Annual Exemption 2021/2022 | £(12,300) |
| Chargeable Gain | £587,700 |
| Tax liability @ 10% | **£58,770** |

# Chapter 7.
# Main Residence Relief

## 59.  Conditions

When an individual sells his or her only or main residence, generally the gain is exempt from capital gains tax (CGT) due to Principal Private Residence (PPR) relief.

The conditions for the relief are that the property must:

- not have been purchased *'wholly or partly'* for the reason of making a gain; and

- be the individual's only or main residence at some point of ownership or claimed to be so; and

- the property is located in the same territory as the 'tax residence' of the individual or the individual must have been resident in the UK for the tax year or have spent at least 90 midnights in the property (see Chapter 5 for detail on 'Non-Resident Landlords').

The last nine months' ownership of a property that has been the individual's only or main residence at some time of ownership is always treated as occupation for the purposes of this relief. This is regardless of whether the taxpayer has actually been resident during those last nine months.

In recognition that a person who is disabled (or their spouse/civil partner) or going into a care home may take longer to sell the residence, the last 36 months are exempt.

## Conditions

Joan bought Rose Cottage on 1 June 2005, living there continuously until she inherited Brook House on 1 January 2008. She stayed at Brook House during the week as it was more convenient for her job, using Rose Cottage as a weekend retreat. Joan sold Rose Cottage on 1 June 2021.

Rose Cottage would be classed as Joan's PPR from 1 June 2005 to 31 December 2007 PLUS she would be allowed the 9 months from 1 September 2020 to the date of sale on 1 June 2021.

Rose Cottage would not qualify for PPR relief for the period 2 January 2008 to 31 August 2020.

The annual exempt amount of £12,300 for 2021/22 would be available for deduction from any profit that might be chargeable.

# 60.  'Residence' - Meaning

Legislation does not define exactly what constitutes a 'residence' but in the tax case of *Batey v Wakefield (1981)55TC550* it was decided that not only can the main residence comprise more than one building but it can also include ancillary buildings that are used as houses in their own right (e.g. summerhouse, staff bungalow).

In the subsequent case of *Williams v Merrylees* (1987)BTC 393 the judge went further stating that *"what one is looking for is an entity which can be sensibly described as being a dwelling-house though split up into different buildings performing different function".*

## 'Residence' – Meaning

A taxpayer purchased a small estate including a lodge sited approximately 200 metres from the main house. The lodge was occupied by a married couple who worked on the estate. The taxpayer sold the main house but retained the lodge after he moved.

When the occupants of the lodge died the taxpayer sold the lodge to the purchasers of the main house.

The commissioners found that the lodge was in the area of the main house and allowed the PPR relief claim.

# 61.   Proving PPR Status (1)

When deciding whether a property should be given Principal Private Residence (PPR) status HMRC will look at whether the owner had any *intention* of living in the property. It is a matter of fact whether a property is the PPR or not but to allow a PPR claim HMRC will require proof that the property has actually been lived in as the PPR.

In *Metcalf v HMRC (2010) UKSC 15,* lack of both oral and other evidence, including lack of consumption of electricity helped the Tribunal find in favour of HMRC.

## Proving PPR Status (1)

Mr Metcalfe owned several properties but claimed one property as his PPR. The property was purchased 'off plan' and came with various fixtures and fittings (carpets, fridge, cooker, etc.).

As proof of non-permanence HMRC stated that no telephone had been installed but Mr Metcalfe argued that he always used his mobile; additional proof was required.

HMRC particularly cited the electricity bill showing low usage over the winter period suggesting non-residence. Mr Metcalfe argued that the bill was low because the apartment was new, had full double-glazing and he worked long shifts.

He insisted that he had purchased the property with the intention of living there permanently but his work took him elsewhere. The Tribunal found that Mr Metcalfe had lived there for a time but could find no proof of *'permanence, continuity and expectation of continuity of occupation'* (following the case of *Goodwin v Curtis (1988 70TC478)* as the evidence was flimsy and more concrete evidence was lacking.

# 62.   Proving PPR Status (2)

As well as there being an *'intention'* to occupy there must be a *'degree of permanence or continuity, or some expectation of continuity'* in order for PPR relief to be allowed. There is no minimum period of occupation that required before the property can amount to a residence as each case turns on its own facts.

However, actions such as registering the new PPR address with the local doctor, on the electoral role, local council, bank etc promptly on moving in would be good evidence that the move was *'intended'* to be long term.

In *Kothari v HMRC (2006) UKFTT TC04915* it was decided that the occupation of a property was not sufficient to qualify it as a residence.

## Proving PPR Status (2)

Mr Kothari purchased a flat in 2005, initially renting out the property. The family moved into the property in January 2009. Mr Kothari elected for the property to be his PPR. The property was sold in July 2009 and Mr Kothari claimed CGT exemption as the PPR.

HMRC refused the claim on the basis that although the occupation was for just over six months, there was not the degree of 'permanence' needed to be deemed the PPR.

HMRC highlighted a number of factors to support their view including:

- That Mr Kothari had only actually occupied the property for a few months before it was sold.

- He had not moved any furniture from his former home into the property but instead bought the previous tenants' furniture.

- Neither his bank nor DVLA were informed of the move.

- Most importantly, in a telephone call with HMRC in 2013 HMRC recorded that Mr Kothari stated that he had retained his former home temporarily whist waiting to see if his family enjoyed living at the flat which, in HMRC's view, indicated that no final decision had been made to live permanently at the flat. The claim was refused.

# 63.   Non-Residents And Main Residence Relief

Non-residents investing in UK residential property and UK residents investing in non-UK property must satisfy a 'day count test' in relation to that property. An owner will be eligible for Principal Private Residence (PPR) relief only if he or she was tax resident in the same country as the property for the relevant tax year or, if non-resident, that he or she spent at least 90 midnights in the property, or in other properties in the same country in the tax year. Spouses and civil partners can only have one residence between them and residence by one spouse/civil partner will be deemed to the residence of the other.

Non-residents are able to nominate that a UK property meeting the 90-day rule is their main residence for the tax year of sale.

The rules mean that individuals who are resident in the UK will remain eligible for PPR but non-residents will need to meet the 90- day rule. UK residents who have overseas property will also need to satisfy the 90-day rule even if they have already elected for the second home overseas to be their main residence for PPR.

Individuals who retire abroad but keep their homes in the UK, are entitled to PPR for the years which they were in the UK, but will be subject to the 90-day rule thereafter for each tax year (apart from the last 9 months of ownership).

Gains attributed to periods before 6 April 2015 are not counted and the non-UK resident is able to 'rebase' the property to the 6 April 2015 market value or, if more beneficial, can either time-apportion the gain or have the entire gain/loss taken into account.

Should a PPR election have been made in respect of a property but the property no longer qualifies for PPR because the residence and day count tests are not met during the 2020/21 year, it will be necessary for a new election to be made for another property, prior to 5 April 2022, to avoid PPR being wasted.

## Non-Residents And Main Residence Relief

Julienne is resident in France and owns a flat in London. In 2021/22 she stayed 80 midnights. Her husband John accompanies her on 30 of those nights. He stayed on for an extra 12 midnights on business.

Julienne passes the 90 'midnights test' because the property has been occupied by one of them for 92 midnights.

If John stays on for only nine extra midnights the test will fail because the property will have been occupied for only 89 midnights.

# 64.  'Flipping'

As long as the initial election for Principal Private Residence (PPR) relief has been made, it can then be varied ('flipped') as many times as desired by submitting a further election. There is no prescribed form or wording for the election, but it must be made within two years of the initial change in *combination of residences'*. Should the two- year time limit be missed, there needs to be a 'trigger' event in order to reset the election date.

Examples of 'trigger' events that could be used to change the *'combination of residences'* are:

- Marriage/civil partnership – both parties owning property used as their respective residence, or where there is joint ownership. Married couples/civil partners can only have one main residence qualifying for PPR such that any election made must be made jointly.

- Renting out one of the properties – when the letting comes to an end the owner can then take up residence.

- Selling half of one residence such that the seller is no longer in full ownership but is still in residence.

- Transferring ownership of a main residence into a trust under which the owner has a beneficial interest, with the proviso that the owner remains in residence. Care is needed so as not to be caught under the 'gift with reservation of benefit' or 'pre-owned asset' rules (see Tips 82 and 83).

PPR is a valuable tax relief and 'flipping' is legitimate tax planning. However, if used too many times or in quick succession, there is the danger that HMRC may investigate in an attempt to prove that either the PPR exemption is invalid and that the real reason for nominating the properties is avoidance of tax or that the owner should be taxed under the income tax rather than CGT rules as a 'serial seller'.

### 'Flipping'

John's main residence is in Woking; his father lives in Camberley. John's father dies and leaves his house to John, who lives in it at weekends.

John is unaware of the election required and misses the election date. Three years after his father's death the election has still not been made.

John marries Jane and the property is transferred into joint ownership. On marriage the election can be made.

# 65.    Delay In Occupation

There is a limited concession to extend Principal Private Residence (PPR) relief should the owner not move into his or her only or main residence on purchase. This covers situations where the owner:

- buys land on which the house is to be built;

- has the house altered or redecorated before moving in; *or*

- remains in the first property whilst it is still on the market, provided that when that property is sold the second property becomes the owner's only or main residence.

In these circumstances, the period before occupation is allowed as PPR providing that the period between acquisition and actual occupation is 12 months or less. This period may be extended to a maximum of two years, but only if HMRC is satisfied there is a good reason for the delay in occupation.

If the effect of this relief means that the owner temporarily has two PPR properties, an election is not required, and relief will be available for both residences for that period.

| Delay In Occupation |
| :---: |

Jim purchased 1 Back Lane on 1 January 1991 as his PPR. On 1 June 2019 he purchased 1 Front Lane intending to live there and rent Back Lane.

Unfortunately, whilst undertaking some building work he discovered that Front Lane was deemed unsafe and returned to live in Back Lane whilst the repair work was being undertaken. The building work took

18 months and then Jim then moved into Front Lane. Front Lane was sold on 1 June 2021.

PPR is granted for the full period of ownership.

# 66.  'Deemed' Occupation

There may be times when the owner is prevented from living in his or her main residence for reasons that are not the owner's by choice. It would be unfair for him or her not to be eligible for Principal Private Residence (PPR) relief for that period of absence.

'Deemed' occupation is only possible where the taxpayer is absent from the property and has no other residence eligible for PPR.

There is no minimum period of occupation for PPR relief but usually the house has to be physically occupied as a residence before and after any period of absence. Should the reason for the absence be that the owner was working away, then he or she does not have to return to the house if work subsequently requires residence elsewhere.

Absences can be cumulative as long as one of three conditions applies:

1.  any period of absence – maximum three years, *or*

2.  overseas employment (not self-employment) of the owner or spouse/civil partner – unlimited period, *or*

3.  employment elsewhere (employed or self-employed) of the owner or spouse/civil partner – maximum four years.

## 'Deemed' Occupation

Stephen has a PPR property in Surrey but has worked in Wales for six years. His mother lives in Scotland and has recently become ill. Stephen intends to take unpaid leave from his job and be her carer.

He can do so for just one year in order to retain PPR on his Surrey property under the 'deemed occupation' rules.

His six years working in Wales have used:

- Condition (3) – four years – employment elsewhere in the UK.

- Condition (1) – two years – any period. Leaving one year available under condition (1).

# 67.    Conversion Of Property

Should a property that was initially a main residence be converted into flats and sold, Principal Private Residence (PPR) relief will be denied in respect of the gain attributable to the period of ownership whilst the conversion had taken place as the expenditure had been incurred *'wholly or partly'* for the purposes of realising a gain. For the calculation a valuation of the property as not converted is required and then that figure is compared with the sale price post conversion in order to establish the additional profit attributable to the conversion.

## Conversion Of Property

Tony lived in a property as his main residence from the date of purchase in July 2000 (cost = £100,000) to July 2016 when work commenced on conversion into three flats. Work was completed in December 2015, the flats finally all being sold in December 2021 for £250,000 each. The conversion cost was £150,000. If the property had remained as one house the sale proceeds would have been £550,000.The additional expenditure for conversion generated an additional gain of £50,000 calculated as follows:

|  | Total Gain | Exempt PPR Gain | Taxable Gain |
|---|---|---|---|
| Proceeds/valuation | £750,000 | £550,000 | £200,000 |
| Original cost of property | £(100,000) | £(100,000) | |
| Conversion expenditure | £(150,000) | | £(150,000) |
| Gain | £500,000 | £450,000 | **£50,000** |

Less annual exemption, if available.

## 68.   PPR And Dependent Relative Relief

Principal Private Residence (PPR) relief cannot be claimed on the sale of a property purchased as the residence of an elderly or infirm ('dependent') relative.

'Dependent relative' is defined as being the owner's own or their spouse/civil partner's widowed or separated mother or any other relative who is unable to look after themselves. PPR is allowed on the proportion of gain made on the property used by the relative pre-5 April 1988, providing that the relative was the property's sole resident, living there rent-free and continuing to do so until three years before sale.

Should there have been a change of occupant after 5 April 1988 the exemption is not allowed for the period after the change to the date of sale, even if the new occupant is another dependent relative.

### PPR And Dependent Relative Relief

David acquired a property on 1 June 1991, selling it on 1 December 2021 realising a gain of £250,000. The house was provided rent-free and without any other consideration as the sole residence of David's widowed mother from the date of acquisition to 1 December 1996 when she died. David's elderly mother-in-law then took up residence.

Total ownership:

| | |
|---|---|
| 1 June 1991 – 1 December 2021 | = 354 months |
| Sole residence of dependent relative: 1 June 1991 – 1 December 1996 | = 54 months |
| Final period (last 18 months exempt) | = 9 months |

PPR relief allowed:

<u>54 months + 18 months</u> x £250,000 354          = £44,491
months

Chargeable gain:

£250,000 less PPR of £44,491                        = **<u>£205,509.</u>**

Less annual exemption, if available.

# 69. Job-Related Accommodation

Where a taxpayer owns a property as his or her main residence but is obliged to live elsewhere in job-related accommodation, the property could be deemed not eligible for Principal Private Residence relief. However, the relief will apply when, during the period of ownership the taxpayer:

- resides in other job-related accommodation; and

- intends to occupy the first property as his or her only or main residence at some time.

This 'job-related' provision is only possible if it is necessary or customary for the employee to live in accommodation provided by the employer for the better performance of their duties – it must not simply be a matter of choice.

The relief is allowed even if the first property is not occupied due to a change of circumstances, provided it has been the *intention* to occupy the property.

## Job-Related Accommodation

Susan occupied her main residence Summer Lodge, Exmouth in Devon until 2005 when her work required her to move into qualifying job-related accommodation in Scotland.

In 2010 she was sent to work in the Devon office but occupied privately rented accommodation.

In 2021 Summer Lodge was sold, not having been re-occupied or let out. Until 2015 she had intended to return to her main residence.

PPR relief is allowed:

1. until 2005 before the move to Scotland;

2. for the period of job-related accommodation between 2005 to 2010;

3. for 2010 to 2012 - 2 years - as a permitted period of absence (see Tip 65); *and*

4. for the final nine months.

# 70. 'Permitted Area'

There is a restriction on the size of garden or grounds attached to a main residence that can be granted Principal Private Residence (PPR) relief.

'Garden or grounds' is not defined in the legislation nor is there binding judicial authority and as such the words take their ordinary meaning. If the garden has been used for other purposes (e.g. commercial woodland, agriculture or trade) then no PRR will be available. Similarly, land which is fenced off for development will also not qualify.

The 'permitted area' must not exceed half a hectare (approximately 1.25 acres); this area is the total area, including the grounds on which the residence is built. However, a larger area may be permitted should it prove to be needed for the 'reasonable enjoyment' of the house as a residence, commensurate with the size and character of the property.

In cases where the land exceeds the permitted area, a District Valuer would be required to give his opinion by applying an objective test. The Judge in the Tribunal case of *Phillips & Anor [2020] TC 07859* (see Tax Case 1 below) stated that whether the 'garden' is permitted must be *'based on what is required by a typical person for 'reasonable enjoyment' of the property by reference to the particular* property, *rather than the particular* owner'.

Care must be taken as to the order of sale – if the residence is sold before the land, then CGT will be charged as the land will no longer be 'attached' to the residence (see Tax Case two below - *Varty v Lynes [1976] 51TC419*).

If the residence plus part of the 'permitted' area is sold then that area will qualify for PPR. However, if the remaining land is sold after the residence then the subsequent sale will not qualify for PPR relief.

If land in grounds larger than half a hectare is sold before the property and PPR is claimed, HMRC will want to know what has changed such that land necessary for the 'reasonable enjoyment' of the house before sale was not required afterwards.

## 'Permitted Area'

**Tax case 1:**

*Phillips & Anor [2020]* TC 07859

Mr and Mrs Phillips purchased a property in 1997. Together with the gardens the property extended to 0.94 of a hectare. They sold the property to a developer in 2014 and claimed that the entire 0.94 hectares were covered by PPR relief as the whole amount of land was 'required' for the reasonable enjoyment of the property.

In arriving at their conclusion, the Tax Commissioners looked at a number of factors, including at local comparable properties, the size and value of those houses and buildings, the ratio of the gardens and the nature of the property's location. The fact that the property was set in a rural location made it more saleable to somebody who was looking for a large house with a large space.

**Tax Case 2:**

*Varty v Lynes [1976]* 51TC419 Mr Varty purchased a house comprising land of less than one acre. He sold the house with part of the garden and applied for planning permission for the remainder which was sold four years later.

HMRC charged CGT on the second sale and the taxpayer appealed, contending that the land had been 'enjoyed' as part of his main residence and that the gain was PPR exempt.

It was held that PPR did not apply.

# 71.   Working From Home

Principal Private Residence (PPR) relief cannot be claimed for any part of the main residence that is used exclusively for business use.

To protect the PPR exemption, the part of the home that is used for business purposes needs to also be available for private use. For example, a room used as an office from which to run the business during the day could also be used by the taxpayer's children to do their homework in the evening.

Where there is exclusive business use, any gain arising on sale must be apportioned and the proportion relating to exclusive business use will be charged to CGT. However, the gain relating to the use of one room may be below the annual exempt amount and not be charged.

As increasingly more and more taxpayers are working from home or are intending to do so after the Covid 19 pandemic, taxpayers need to be aware of this potential PPR restriction of claim on any future main residence sale.

| Working From Home |
|---|
| Julia runs a marketing business from home. Her home has eight rooms and she uses one exclusively as an office. |
| On the sale of her property on in December 2021, she realises a gain of £95,000. |
| One-eighth (£11,875) would be charged to CGT. |
| To the extent that her annual exemption (£12,300 for 2021/2022) remains available, this would shelter the gain with the result that no CGT would be payable. |

# Chapter 8.
# Gifting Property

## 72.   Gift Between Spouses/Civil Partners

If a gift of a property (or share of a property) is made or a property is sold at less than its market value, CGT is charged as if the donor had received the market value in cash.

This ruling does not apply to transfers (gifts) between spouses/civil partnerships. In such a situation the donee is treated as having acquired the property at the date of the transaction on a 'no gain/ no loss' basis, and most importantly at the original purchase price.

No CGT will be due until the receiving spouse/civil partner sells the property. The transfer must be an outright gift with no conditions attached.

There is nothing to stop the receiving spouse from returning the gift at a later date. However, care needs to be taken in the planning as such transfers could be challenged by HMRC under the *Ramsay* anti-avoidance principle which broadly enables the courts to look behind the individual steps of a transaction to ascertain the legal nature of a series of transactions as a whole. (*W T Ramsay Ltd v IRC [1981] STC 174*).

The situation is different if the property transferred is the Principal Private Residence (PPR). If a person marries and is given a part share of a PPR property owned by the other spouse *after marriage* then the donor inherits the donee spouses' PPR history even though the donee spouse may not have lived there.

## Gift Between Spouses/Civil Partners

Joe is a 45% additional rate taxpayer who owns a Buy To Let property originally purchased for £150,000. He gifts the property to his son on 1 December 2021 when its value is £250,000.

Joe is deemed to have received the market value and as such his CGT tax liability is:

| | |
|---|---|
| Market value less original price | £100,000 |
| Annual Exemption 2021/2022 | £(12,300) |
| Chargeable Gain | £ 87,700 |
| Tax due @ 28% | £ 24,556 |

However, there will be a practical problem in that no monies will have been received out of which to pay the CGT.

If Joe had gifted the property to his wife no CGT would be due on transfer, but should his wife subsequently sell the property, the base value would be the original cost of £150,000.

# 73. Transfer Of Let Property On Separation

The CGT on gifts between spouses as being at *'no gain/no loss'* apply until the end of the tax year of separation. Ideally therefore, the transfer of any jointly held assets should be made some time before the end of the tax year in which separation took place in order to be fully exempt. The asset (which could include the main residence) will be valued as at the date of the gift rather than the 50% share of the original cost. Thus an 'uplift' in the value of the property is achieved which may be beneficial should the property subsequently be sold.

Should the transfer take place after the end of the tax year in which separation occurs but before the granting of the Decree Absolute, then the parties are treated as 'connected parties'; as such the disposal is automatically treated as being at market value whatever the actual amount paid.

## Transfer Of Let Property On Separation

Adam and Eve separated in May 2021. They jointly own a Buy To Let property. Adam transfers the property to Eve in November 2021.

The property originally cost £200,000 with costs of acquisition being £2,500. Legal costs on transfer following separation and paid for by Adam were £2,500.

Adam's deemed disposal proceeds are:

| | |
|---|---|
| Cost (50% share) | £100,000 |
| Acquisition costs (50% share) Legal costs | £1,250 |
| Legal costs | £2,500 |
| Total deemed proceeds | £103,750 |

Eve's revised base cost will be her share (£101,250) plus £103,750 = £205,000.

# 74.  Transfer Of PPR On Separation

When one spouse leaves the marital home it ceases to be the main residence for PPR purposes. On sale, PPR is available for the period of occupation and the last nine months of ownership. Therefore moving out before the final nine months, means a chargeable gain may arise on a disposal.

It is possible to make a claim that the former marital home is the PPR even though one spouse has ceased living there. However this only applies where the property is being disposed of to the ex-spouse, not to anyone else. There are also conditions that apply.

On separation many couples decide that one party is to remain in the main residence and the other party is to leave, transferring their interest to the other rather than immediately selling the property. If the transfer is made during the year of separation, then the PPR relief is not affected should the property be sold at a later date.

Should the sale be after the date of separation, PPR is still available for both parties so long as the property is sold within 9 months after the date of separation and one spouse leaving the family home.

A CGT charge will be triggered by one joint owner's interest not being fully covered by PPR. This situation may arise when, as part of the divorce settlement, the wife is awarded use of the marital home under a *'Mesher'* order, until such time as the children have finished school, the property then being sold, and the proceeds split between the two parties. A *'Mesher'* order is a court order that postpones the sale of the marital home, the actual date of sale being dependent upon certain specified events.

The only situation where HMRC permit more than 9 months is where the property is transferred to the remaining spouse under a *'Mesher'* order

AND an election has not been made by the former spouse for another house to be deemed the PPR.

Of course, if the house is sold after the nine months having not been transferred to the remaining spouse, then CGT will be due on the gain attributable to the spouse who moved out, but only on the proportion of gain in relation to the total period of ownership or 31 March 1982, whichever is the later date made less the nine months.

# 75.    Exchange Of Interests

If a gift of a property is made to a non-spouse/civil partner, CGT is charged on the donor as if the market value of the item had actually been received.

However, in a situation where joint owners of a property wish to become tenants in common such as each owns their own respective part, then provided no money changes hands, a form of 'reinvestment relief' can be applied and no CGT charged. In this scenario the joint owners are treated as if each had sold their share for its market value and then the proceeds 'reinvested' in acquiring the other's half share.

If one of the joint owners pays extra for a higher percentage share then CGT will be charged on the person receiving the additional payment equivalent to the actual amount paid. A similar situation would apply where there are two properties jointly owned but the owners wanted to swap interests so that each owned their own property. If the properties were not of equal value whoever receives the higher value will be subject to a CGT charge.

A significant exception to this relief is if any of the properties is, or has at any time been, a Principal Private Residence (PPR) of one of the owners or later becomes their PPR, such that a disposal within the next six years following exchange is eligible for PPR relief.

However, if the properties involved in the exchange become solely owned PPRs of their respective individual owners then the 'reinvestment' relief may still apply. The 'main residence' problem is that this 'exception to the exception' applies only if all parties' properties are their respective main PPR. Married couples and civil partners count as 'sole' owners in this context.

The situation with regard to Stamp Duty Land Tax under exchange of properties is covered under Tip 98.

## Exchange Of Interests

Alan and Brian (who are not connected persons) jointly own two rental properties, Greengables and Whitegables, respectively. Each property was originally inherited at market value of £50,000 each. They decide to exchange their joint interests such that Alan acquires the sole interest in Greengables and Brian secures exclusive title to Whitegables.

At the time of exchange Greengables has a market value of £200,000; Whitegables has a value of £250,000. No cash changes hands, but Brian has obtained the more valuable interest, and therefore greater proceeds, for the disposal of his share.

Cost for future CGT purposes = Cost of original ½ share + deemed cost of ½ share in exchange.

Alan's calculation:

| | |
|---|---|
| MV consideration | £100,000 |
| Less cost | £(25,000) |
| Less 'reinvestment' | £(75,000) |
| Gain | NIL |

Brian's calculation:

| | |
|---|---|
| MV consideration | £125,000 |
| Less cost | £(25,000) |
| Less 'reinvestment' | £(75,000) |
| Chargeable Gain on exchange | £ 25,000 |

Less annual exemptions, if available.

Cost for future CGT purposes for both properties:

£25,000 + £25,000 = £50,000.

# 76.   'Value Shifting'

'Value shifting' occurs when the value of a property is altered as a result of the passing of an interest in the property to another.

Anti-avoidance rules are in place whereby such disposals are deemed to be chargeable to CGT where no consideration involved. In these situations, the 'market value' rule is deemed to operate and the person transferring the value is liable to CGT based on the amount which he or she could have obtained for the transfer, if the parties had been at arm's length.

The main situations where these anti-avoidance rules operate are where the owner of a freehold property effectively changes the type of ownership by disposing of the freehold whilst granting a leasehold, thereby reducing the value of the property. However, the calculation recognises that the property will revert to the freeholder at the end of the lease and at the date of leasehold creation is taxed as a part disposal where:

- A is the premium received or value transferred, and
- B is the residual value retained by the landlord plus the value of the right to receive the any rent.

Any subsequent alteration to the lease will automatically result in a CGT charge despite no consideration been received.

Should the lease be granted at a premium a proportion will be taxed as income tax using the calculation: Premium less the premium × (no. of years of the lease − 1).

## 'Value Shifting'

David owns a commercial property currently valued at £200,000 with an original purchase price of £120,000. If he gifts the property to his son, with no consideration, the transaction would be treated as if he had sold at the 'market value' as the two are 'connected persons'. Instead he gives the freehold to his son, granting himself a lease for 99 years at a rent of £1 per year. The value of the freehold will be negligible.

He then arranges for the lease to be altered so that the rent is at the market rate resulting in the increase in value of the freehold.

The change in the terms of the lease is an example of 'value shifting' because the lease itself has become less valuable but the freehold more valuable.

At the date of alteration David will be charged to CGT on the basis that he has disposed of an asset equal to the value transferred. If the value of the £1 per year lease was £200,000 and the 'market value' lease £60,000, the value transferred would be £140,000.

The corresponding deductible cost is calculated in proportion to the value deemed to be transferred (£140,000), against the original value (£200,000).

| | |
|---|---|
| £140,000 x £120,000 = £200,000 | £ 84,000 |
| Capital Gains calculation: | |
| Deemed Proceeds | £140,000 |
| Less value transferred | £(84,000) |
| Chargeable Gains | £ 56,000 |

Less annual exemption, if available.

# 77.   'Hold-Over' Relief

'Hold-over' relief is a way of deferring payment of CGT on certain assets, including land and buildings used in a business, until the new owner of the asset sells.

The donee, in effect, takes over the original cost of the asset and may eventually have to pay CGT on both the gain incurred from the date of gift plus the gain 'held over'.

HMRC have produced Help Sheet 295 *'Relief of gifts and similar transactions'* that details the procedure. A claim form needs to be signed and submitted. The Help Sheet can be downloaded at:

www.gov.uk/government/publications/relief-for-gifts-and-similar-transactions-hs295-self-assessment-helpsheet (updated Nov 2020).

| 'Hold-Over' Relief |
|---|
| Judy owns a second home which shows a significant gain. She gives the cottage to her husband Jim. |
| This is treated as a 'no gain/no loss' disposal between them as they are married. Jim is treated as acquiring the cottage for the price that Judy paid originally (so preserving the gain in his hands), as from the date of the inter-spouse disposal. |
| Jim manages the property as a qualifying furnished holiday let and after a year gives the property to their adult daughter, Louise, claiming 'hold-over' relief so that Louise takes over her mother's historic base cost. |

Louise subsequently occupies the property as her only or main residence such that when the property is sold Principal Private Residence relief will reduce the gain chargeable.

# 78.   'Incorporation Relief'

Should a property letting business be run by one or more individuals who wish to transfer the property into a limited company then there will be a CGT charge on the transfer at market value as the parties are deemed to be 'connected'.

The charge can be wholly or partly postponed by use of 'incorporation relief' (a form of 'hold-over') where the exchange is wholly or partly for shares in the company. The charge is deferred until the person transferring the business disposes of the company shares; then the 'held-over' gain is deducted from the cost of the shares resulting in an increased charge when the shares are eventually sold.

'Incorporation relief' applies if:

- a person who is not a company (i.e. sole trader, partner) transfers a business as a going concern into a company;

- together with the whole assets of the business (excluding cash as this is not a CGT chargeable asset); *and*

- the business is so transferred wholly or partly in exchange for shares issued by the company to the person transferring the business.

HMRC's *Extra-Statutory Concession (ESC) D32* indicates that relief is still available should some or all of the liabilities of the business not be taken over by the company.

The relief is mandatory and automatic and therefore does not require a claim (although the person transferring the business can elect for the relief not be apply).

Although the claim is automatic HMRC are increasingly challenging any claim for relief. The tax case of *Ramsay v HMRC [2013]* shows how difficult it can be to succeed with this claim as one of the conditions is the definition of 'business' rather than the rental being an 'investment' activity.

## 'Incorporation' Relief

The taxpayer was the landlord of a large property which had been converted into ten flats, five of which were occupied by tenants.

The property was transferred to a company, in exchange for shares in that company under an 'incorporation relief' claim.

HMRC initially disallowed the claim arguing that the letting and administration of property was an investment activity and as such there was no 'qualifying business'.

The taxpayer appealed and the court allowed this particular claim, finding that the activities performed in the letting were over and above those which were incidental to the owning of an investment property.

# Chapter 9.
# Inheritance Tax Planning

# 79.  Inheritance Tax Charge

Inheritance tax (IHT) can be relevant on chargeable lifetime transfers of assets (termed 'potential exempt' transfers) such as rental property (e.g. gifts into most types of trust) and on the net value (assets less liabilities) of an estate of death (which may include property). On death the first £325,000 is exempt (the 'nil rate band') with the balance being taxed at 40% (2021/22). An additional exempt amount is available ('Residence Nil Rate Band) for those estates where the deceased owned a residence (or has downsized) and that residence has been inherited by the deceased's children or other lineal descendants (e.g. grandchildren) – see Tip 80.

If a gift of property is made to someone who is not in a marriage/civil partnership with the donor, this 'potentially exempt' transfer will only be chargeable to IHT should the donor not survive seven years. This exemption will not apply if the property gifted has conditions attached (termed a *'Gift With Reservation Of Benefit'* - see Tips 82 and 83).

Individuals domiciled in the UK are liable to IHT on chargeable worldwide property. Non-UK domiciled individuals are also liable to IHT, but only on chargeable UK property.

Transfers between spouses/civil partners who are resident in the UK are exempt from IHT. Therefore, if property is left to the surviving spouse/civil partner there will be no IHT due on the first death, but there may be on the second death, depending on whether the estate is in excess of £650,000 (2 x £325,000) and the 'Residence Nil Rate Band' is available (see Tip 80).

Property placed within a 'Discretionary' ('Mainstream') trust does not normally form part of the donor's estate on death unless the settlor or their spouse/civil partner benefits from income or gains from assets held within the trust.

# 80.   Residence Nil Rate Band

Where a residence forms part of an estate or the deceased downsized after 8 July 2015 such that the value has reduced there is an additional 'Residence Nil Rate Band' (RNRB) available to a maximum of £175,000 for 2021/22.

The RNRB can only be used to shelter IHT on one residential property. Where there is more than one such property that has been a main residence at some point, the personal representatives can nominate which property that passed on death will benefit from the RNRB.

RNRB is only available to estates where the residence is bequeathed to the deceased's children and other lineal descendants. This means that those without children or cohabitees where a child is of the other cohabitee are disadvantaged.

Both the Nil Rate Band (NRB) and RNRB are transferable between spouses either in whole or in part. The amount of any transfer of the RNRB is not a fixed amount but rather the percentage of the RNRB which is not used by the first spouse to die, used to reduce the amount of the RNRB at the date of death of the surviving spouse.

The transfer of unused RNRB is not automatic and must be claimed within two years of the date of death.

**'Downsizing'**

The RNRB band is preserved where the deceased has 'downsized' such that:

- the property disposed was owned by the deceased and would have qualified for the RNRB had the deceased still owned it at death;

- the property is of less value, or other assets of an equivalent value if the property has been disposed of, are in the deceased's estate;

- the property is left to direct descendants of the deceased; *and*

- the 'downsizing' event was on or after 8 July 2015.

This measure ensures that an estate remains eligible for the proportion of the NRB foregone as a result of downsizing or selling the residence. This 'additional' RNRB and the RNRB available on death in respect of any residence left to direct descendants cannot exceed the RNRB for the tax year in which death occurred.

## Residence Nil Rate Band

Betty was widowed in May 2021.

In July 2021, she sells the family home for £500,000, and moves into a flat which costs £200,000. If she had died before the move, her estate would have been entitled to use the RNRB of £175,000 plus 100% of the unused RNRB inherited from her late husband – a further £175,000 giving her a total available RNRB of £350,000 (plus any unused NRB and transferable NRB of late husband). By downsizing, she has potentially lost the chance to use £150,000 (£350,000 - £200,000) of the RNRB. This is 42.85 % of the available RNRB at the time she downsized.

Betty dies in March 2022. At the time of her death, her flat is worth £210,000. She leaves this, with the remainder of her estate worth £700,000 to her only daughter, Julie. The estate is able to use a RNRB of £210,000 to shelter the property from IHT. She is also able to benefit from the 'downsizing' addition. 'Additional' RNRB of £149,975 (i.e. 42.85% of £350,000) is calculated, being the proportion lost as a result of downsizing. However, as the additional RNRB (£149,975) and the RNRB (£210,000) together (£359,975) exceed the RNRB for the

2021/21 tax year of £350,000 (2 x £175,000), the additional nil rate band is capped at £140,000 (£350,000 less RNRB used of £210,000).

The RNRB and additional RNRB are available on death, together with the nil rate band of £325,000 and any proportion of the nil rate band unused on her late husband's death.

*This example was first printed in Property Tax Insider in January 2016 (updated).*

# 81. 'Related Property'

When the transfer of interest in a property jointly owned takes place (e.g. on death) the value of each individual's joint interest is valued at a discount of the whole. Although ownership of part of the property will entitle the co-owner to reside in the whole property, the Valuation Office has indicated that the person's share could be eligible for a potential discount of 10–15% on the freehold vacant possession value (depending upon the specifics of the situation).

However, HMRC have special valuation rules for 'related property' which apply where the value of each half produces a higher value than a normal discounted valuation of the whole. The interests of each owner will usually be identical and extend to the entire property such that *'the value of the deceased/transferor's interest will be the appropriate proportion of the entirety value.'*

There are two methods of calculation being the 'general rule' and 'special rule'. The general rule is the one usually used in a freehold/leasehold property valuation situation. The special rule is mainly used for calculating the value of shareholdings where the value of the same shares can vary with the size of holding.

If 'related property' is sold to an unconnected person within three years of death for less than the related property valuation, at an 'arm's length', for a price freely negotiated to a seller who has no connection to the seller or deceased then a claim is available to substitute that valuation with the value it would have been had the 'related property' rules did not apply.

The relief must be claimed within four years after the date that the original IHT charge was paid.

## 'Related Property'

Blackacre and Whiteacre are adjacent parcels of land owned respectively by the deceased and his wife. Their separate values are £40,000 and £10,000. But because of the relationship between the two parcels of land – one has no access without the other – they together make a natural unit valued at £80,000.

On the deceased's death the value of Blackacre is:

(£40,000 ÷ £50,000) × £80,000 = £64,000

*Example taken from HMRC Manual IHTM09735*

# 82.   Gift With Reservation Of Benefit (1)

The ideal in inheritance tax lifetime planning would be for the donor to gift the main residence out of the estate but at the same time remain living in the property. However, the 'Gift With Reservation Of Benefit' (GWRB) rules do not allow a simple transfer of a whole or even part of a property to another whilst the donor remains in residence (i.e. *reserves a benefit*). If such a transaction does take place then the property is treated as remaining within the donor's estate on death.

Gifts during an individuals' lifetime are 'Potentially Exempt Transfers' ('PET') only coming into charge should the donor die within seven years of the transfer. The GWRB rules ensure that should the donor survive the seven years that the PET does not become an exempt transfer.

With specific reference to land, the gift would be treated as a GWRB if there is some interest, right or arrangement allowing the donor to occupy and *enjoy the land concerned to a material degree'*. HMRC regard a 'right' as the donor being entitled or enabled to occupy all or part of the land otherwise than for full consideration (i.e. unless full market rent is paid by the donor occupier to the donee owner).

A sale of a property to a 'connected person' must be at the full market value otherwise the balance of value is deemed to be a 'gift' and then that 'gifted' value will be included in the donor's estate on death if he or she continues to reside in the property.

## Gift With Reservation Of Benefit (1)

In 2012 James sold a house then worth £100,000 to his adult son, John, for £25,000.

John did not live in the house, but James remained there until he died in 2021.

The disposal is a GWRB and the value of the property gifted was 75% of the total value.

Thus, 75% of the property's value at death is treated as James' property and the value will be liable to IHT.

# 83.    Gift With Reservation Of Benefit (2)

The gift of undivided shares of property will not be subject to the 'Gift With Reservation Of Benefit' (GWRB) rules provided the donor and donee both occupy the property and share expenses. The donor must not receive any benefit from occupation other than a negligible one, which in itself must be paid for by the donor.

It is not necessary for a proportionate sharing of the expenses, but the donor must at least bear the full share of the expenses attributable to him or her (e.g. heating, lighting, council tax etc) that reflects their respective usage and not their respective ownership percentages.

Should the property gifted form part of a donor's final estate under the GWRB rules then the property is treated as being 'inherited' the property for the purposes of the 'Residence Nil Rate Band' (see Tip 80) and be included in the calculation.

### Gift With Reservation Of Benefit (2)

James owns the whole of the house which he occupies with his (adult) daughter and son. James gifts one third of the property to each but continues to live in the property. All three contribute equally to the day-to-day expenses of the property, including the cost of a new kitchen.

If the cost of the new kitchen had been met by the children only, then there would be a GWRB at that date because the owner, James, had received a benefit *'provided by or at the expense of the donee for some reason connected with the gift'* (s104 (b) Finance Act 2004).

A couple of years later James' daughter decides to move out of the property and it is at that date that a GWRB will arise in respect of her share unless James pays a market rent for the continued occupancy of his daughter's one-third share.

# 84.   Pre-Owned Assets Tax

The 'Pre-Owned Assets Tax' (POAT) is an income tax charge levied on the 'benefit' earned on any property that has been given away (or sold for less than its full value) but of which the owner still enjoys the use.

The charge also applies if the owner gives someone the funds to purchase a property, or an interest in it, or owned another property which was sold, and the proceeds gifted to buy the property. The charge will not apply if there is a gap of more than seven years between the gift and the purchase of the property.

The benefit is calculated by reference to the rental value of the property, i.e. the rent that would have been payable if it had been let to the taxpayer at an annual open market rent.

There is a 'de minimus' amount of £5,000 per tax year per spouse/civil partner, but it is not possible to transfer any unused exemption from one partner to the other.

**NOTE:**

1. Either of the Gift With Reservation of Benefit (GWRB – see Tips 82 and 83) or the POAT rules could apply in the situation where a donor has gifted property but remains in residence paying no or minimal rent.

2. If POAT rule apply and it is not viable to meet the ongoing income tax bill but there is less concern about the eventual IHT bill, an election can be made for the GWRB rules to apply instead of the POAT.

## Pre-Owned Assets Tax

### Scenario 1

David gives his son, Jim, £250,000 which he spends on acquiring Greenacres. David moves into Greenacres and will be subject to the POAT charge as from that date.

If the market rent of the property is £4,995 per annum and no rent is paid, there will be no POAT charge as the market rent is less than the 'de minimus' limit.

If the market rent is £10,000 per annum and David is contracted to pay a rent of £5,000, the full £10,000 will be subject to the POAT charge but with a reduction for the rent paid.

### Scenario 2

David moves into a house that Jim had bought with his own money. David gives Jim funds for improvements. There will be no POAT charge because it is not David's money that has been used to acquire the property.

### Scenario 3

David decides to move to Spain and after he sold his property in England, he gave Jim £200,000. Jim used this money to purchase a property. David is now in bad health and returns to England to stay with Jim for three months of the year. As David originally used the money to purchase the property the contribution condition is met during each period of occupation and it will be a question of fact whether he will be seen to be in occupation during the remaining nine months. If, for example, he has a room set aside for him then he will be deemed to be 'in occupation' for the whole year and be subject to the POAT charge.

# 85.   IHT Planning – Selling The Main Residence

**Suggestions to restrict tax liability.**

- Sell the property, downsize and make a cash gift to a donee out of the proceeds. The amount of the gift needs to be sufficient to reduce the taxable estate to below the exempt amount, the remaining money being used to purchase a less costly property. The gift of cash is a deemed potentially exempt transfer (PET) for IHT charge purposes and there will be no 'Gift With Reservation Of Benefit' problems as there is no retained benefit (see Tips 82 and 83). However, the donor does have to live for seven years for the gift to be totally IHT-free.

- Sell the property to a donee for the market price and then lease the property back, paying the full market rent to live there. The monies received could then be gifted in the form of PETs, or spent. Any capital appreciation will accrue to the recipient, the purchase money being raised via a qualifying loan. There would be practical issues such as the seller's security of tenure, stamp duty land tax payable on the sale, the market rent would be subject to income tax in the recipient's hands, and the capital gains tax Principal Private Residence relief might not be available for the recipient on the subsequent sale of the property.

The additional 'Residents Nil Rate Band' (see Tip 80) will be available should an owner downsize or cease to own a main residence and assets of an equivalent value, up to the value of the additional 'nil-rate band', are passed on death to direct descendants.

## 86.    IHT Planning – Gifting The Main Residence

**Suggestions**

- Gift the property and then pay full market rent to live there. The gift will be a potentially exempt transfer (PET); income tax on the rent will be paid by the donee.

- Mortgage the house, giving away the proceeds or invest the money in assets that potentially do not attract IHT, for example AIM shares. After two years, the investments should qualify for 100% relief from inheritance tax. However, mortgage interest will be charged. The funds borrowed could be gifted as a PET.

- Move to a rented property and gift the property. The gift will be a PET. If the gift is made within 18 months of the date of moving no capital gains tax will be charged if the property has been the individual's only or main residence throughout the period of ownership.

**NOTE:** The suggestions above will need to take into account the additional 'Residents Nil Rate Band' (see Tip 80) available should a main residence be passed on death to a direct descendant or the owner downsize or cease to own a main residence and assets of an equivalent value, up to the value of the additional 'nil-rate band', are passed on death to direct descendants.

# 87.   Sales Post Death

Beneficiaries under a deceased's will are deemed to inherit the assets at market value as at the date of death. However, if a property is sold within four years of death at a lower price than the value used for the probate value used for the IHT calculation on the estate, that earlier IHT liability can be reduced by substituting the lower sale proceeds for the agreed value, therefore saving the estate IHT.

The relief is known as '*loss on sale of land relief*' and should more than one property be sold in the four years after death, then the sale price of all those properties is substituted for the values at death.

Where relief is claimed, the sale price must be substituted for the probate value for all properties sold within the four-year period. The executors cannot choose the value which gives the best result – the same approach must be applied consistently.

This relief is not available where either:

- the difference between the date of death value and the sale price is less than £1,000 or 5% of the value on death, whichever is the lower; or

- the sale is to the spouse/civil partner, children or remoter descendants, trustees or a person who had an interest in the property at any time between death and the date of sale.

## Sales Post Death

Molly died in September 2018 owning a property valued for IHT purposes at £400,000. The property was eventually sold to a third party for £360,000 in 2021.

The loss on the probate value is:

£400,000 − £360,000 = £(40,000).

Depending upon the value of the estate, up to £16,000 IHT can be refunded.

Calculation: £40,000 @ 40% = £16,000.

# 88.  Furnished Holiday Lets – Business Property Relief

Business Property Relief (BPR) provides relief from IHT and is available on the transfer of certain types of business assets subject to a minimum ownership period. The transfer can be made during a person's lifetime or on their death. For BPR to apply the business must be carried on with the view of making a profit and be run on sound business principles.

For income tax and capital gains tax purposes the operation of a furnished holiday let (FHL) is treated as a business and as such BRP should be available on sale. However, invariably such a claim does not succeed because HMRC will argue that there are not enough services being provided by the owners to make the FHL an 'active' business. Their stance is that ultimately FHL is purely land rental and for a BPR claim to succeed there needs to be shown a higher level of services given.

The case of *The Personal Representatives of Grace Joyce Graham v HMRC [2018] UKFTT 0306 (TC)*, shows the level of services required for a claim to succeed and the method by which the Tribunal reached their decision.

## Furnished Holiday Lets - Business Property Relief

The deceased lived in a farmhouse and provided accommodation in four self-contained self-catering flats or cottages which were part of the building.

HMRC disallowed the claim to BPR on the grounds that the business was not relevant business property but an investment.

The Tribunal disagreed and in reaching their decision they considered:

- *looking at all the components of the business separately, would an intelligent businessman view the business as mainly the holding of investments?; and*

- *if an element is identified which has a substantial investment component, do the other non-investment components outweigh it?*

The Tribunal members agreed that the taking payments from guests in exchange for accommodation, advertising, taking bookings and repairing and maintaining the buildings, could be described as investment activities.

However, there were other aspects which could not e.g. the fact that the deceased and her daughter worked 200 hours a week between them during peak season providing additional services such as home-made and purchased food and drink including fresh fish, maintaining the swimming pool, sauna, herb garden and arranging numerous leisure activities.

# Chapter 10.
# The Use Of Trusts

# 89.    The Basics Of Trusts

**What is a trust?**

A trust is created when a person (a 'settlor') transfers assets to people whom they 'trust' ('trustees') to hold them on behalf of others ('beneficiaries').

**Why use a trust?**

*   *Convenience* – the beneficiary may be a minor who is unable, as yet, to take responsibility for the property themselves, or the settlor may be looking for flexibility to provide for a class of beneficiaries who might not even be born at the time the trust is created (such as grandchildren).

*   *Reduce taxation* – property placed within a 'Discretionary' trust does not normally form part of the settlor's estate on death (unless the trust is one where the settlor retains an interest) and as such this reduces any inheritance tax that may be due.

*   *Protect the property* — this is the main reason that trusts are created – in case:

    -    the beneficiary turns out to be someone who cannot manage the property themselves, *or*
    -    the property would otherwise need to be sold to pay for long-term care, *or*
    -    to protect the property from potential bankruptcy or divorce.

**Different types of trust**

1.  Qualifying 'Interest in Possession' (QIIP) trusts; *and*

2.  'Discretionary' trusts (also known as 'Relevant Property Trusts') such as:

    *   'Nil rate band' trusts.
    *   'Charge' trusts.

Under a QIIP trust, a beneficiary is entitled to the income generated by the underlying property held within the trust whereas with a 'Discretionary' trust no one person is absolutely entitled to the income, rather it is at the *discretion* of the trustees as to the distribution dependent upon the terms of the Trust Deed.

Trust planning is for the long term and can be used to secure assets, including property, which are likely to grow in value.

## The Basics Of Trusts

**NOTE:** Trust planning is specialist work and should only be undertaken by someone who is qualified to give such advice.

# 90.   'Interest In Possession' Trust

**How does it work?**

- The beneficiary has the right to receive an income for a defined period from the trust (usually for the remainder of the beneficiary's life) but not the right to the capital held within the trust. Thus, rented property can produce the income but the property itself remains within the trust.

- The 'interest' will cease when a beneficiary becomes *'absolutely entitled'* to the trust assets either on a death for example, on the death of a surviving parent or when some special condition is met (e.g. upon reaching a specified age, say, 18 years)). On being absolutely entitled the beneficiary can direct the trustees as to how to deal with the property; the beneficiary may even require the property to be transferred to him or her.

**Advantages**

- 'Interest in possession' trusts are a potentially useful way of providing a safe income for dependents of the settlor, whilst ensuring that the property is saved to be passed on at a later date.

- On the death of someone who has an 'interest in possession', the 'interest' comes to an end and the beneficiary becomes absolutely entitled to the trust property, but no CGT is due (but neither are any capital losses allowable).

- A chargeable gain will only arise to the trust if the cost of the property had been reduced by 'hold-over' relief on transfer into the trust, the gain being equal to the amount 'held-over'.

# 91.   'Nil Rate Band' Trust

**How does it work?**

• A 'nil rate band' (NRB) 'Discretionary' trust is created on death in a sum equal in value to the inheritance tax NRB (£325,000 for 2021/22) or the settlor's unused NRB if already part-used.

• The trust can comprise a property.

• Each spouse/civil partner must own the property as 'tenants in common'.

• If the home is held in a trust before a person dies and it stays in trust when they die, then the property can qualify for the additional 'Residents Nil Rate Band' if it becomes part of the direct descendant's estate after the person dies (see Tip 80).

• Each spouse/civil partner must own the property as 'tenants in common'.

• The surviving spouse has the legal right to occupy the property by virtue of ownership of their own half-share.

• The trustees are deemed to own a beneficial 50% share of the property which is effectively subject to a sitting tenant; the property cannot be sold because they do not entirely own it.

**Advantages**

• Maximum flexibility over the estate; spouse IHT exemption retained, although this point is less relevant now the unused IHT allowance of the first spouse to die is transferable to the surviving spouse.

• No problems should a beneficiary become bankrupt or die.

- If sold, capital gains tax Principal Private Residence relief is potentially available on the value of the property as a whole.

- The remaining estate assets can be left outright.

- Assets held in trust are not assessed as capital of the surviving spouse for long-term care.

- Guarantee that the trust assets pass per the donor's wishes.

# 92.   'Charge' Trust

'Charge trusts' may be relevant should it be desired to place assets within a trust for the children up to the Nil Rate Band (NRB). However, this may leave the surviving spouse short of assets in a smaller estate where, perhaps, the house is the main asset. In this situation the whole or part of the gift could be secured by a charge on the property in favour of the trustees and could be interest free and payable on demand.

**How does it work?**

- The 'Discretionary' trust is created on the first spouse/civil partner's death by placing his or her share of the property into the trust.

- At the trustees' discretion the loan monies are given to the remaining spouse/civil partner as beneficiary. The loan is kept by the trustees as a debt of the estate until 'called in' on the death of the second spouse.

- The surviving spouse will normally have no personal liability for the charge which can be index-linked to take into account future increases in the IHT NRB.

- Alternatively, the charge can be expressed as a proportion of the value of the property calculated periodically thereby benefiting from any capital appreciation, or be made to track a publicly available index of property prices for comparable properties.

- On the second death the loan from the trust is repaid out of their estate. The NRB is applied to the remainder of the estate assets.

**Advantages**

- The property remains owned by the surviving spouse who benefits from either the capital gains tax Principal Private Residence relief should the property be subsequently sold, or a base cost uplift if retained until death.

- On the death of the surviving spouse IHT will be payable but reduced by the charge and, if calculated correctly, to below the NRB.

## 93.   CGT 'Hold-Over' Relief

On the transfer of property into a trust, the original owner of the property (the 'settlor') is treated as having gifted the property to the trust at market value for CGT purposes. The 'market value' rule applies because the settlor and trust are deemed to be 'connected' when the trust comes into existence.

If the property transferred has increased in value since the date of the settlor's acquisition, then the settlor will have a chargeable gain and possibly CGT to pay. However, the settlor can claim to defer ('hold-over') the charge if the trust has been created whilst the settlor is alive (assets transferred into a trust on death do not attract CGT).

'Hold-over' relief is a way to defer the payment of CGT until the trust sells the property. The relief is not available should the settlor retain an interest in the property transferred.

### CGT 'Hold-Over' Relief

Andy creates a trust whilst he is still alive and transfers two properties into it.

The original total purchase price of the properties was £300,000; the value at the date of transfer into the trust is £500,000 – the gain of £200,000 being 'held-over'.

Four years later the trust sells the properties for £1,000,000. The trust will be liable to tax on a total gain of £700,000 – comprising the gain made whilst the properties were held within the trust and the gain 'held-over'.

# 94.  CGT 'Hold-Over' Relief And PPR

The beneficiary of a trust can live in a property held within a trust as their main residence and on the future disposal of the property Principal Private Residence (PPR) relief will be available.

However, if a 'hold-over' election was made on transfer into the trust PPR is denied on any subsequent sale. This is the position whether the trust sells the property, or the property is transferred out of the trust and then the transferee sells.

Therefore, the choice is between:

1.  paying CGT at the date of transfer into the trust based on the market value and claiming PPR relief on the future sale; *or*

2.  'holding over' the gain on transfer into the trust, but the trust being liable to CGT on the whole gain on the final sale.

### CGT 'Hold-Over' Relief And PPR

Where a property has been subject to a 'hold-over' relief election PPR exemption is no longer available until after it has been sold to a third party.

Consider not electing for 'hold-over' relief into the trust but opting to pay CGT sooner rather than later, especially if it is thought that CGT rates are likely to rise in the future.

# Chapter 11.
# Miscellaneous

# 95. Stamp Duty Land Tax – Individuals

Stamp duty land tax (SDLT) is potentially chargeable whenever a transaction involving land takes place, however effected, unless there is a relief or exemption. The charge is named 'Land and Buildings Transactions Tax' (LBTT) in Scotland and 'Land Transaction Tax' (LTT) in Wales and each have their own respective tax rates.

On an exchange of property (see Tip 75) should one owner receive a larger share of the property but nothing is paid in return then there is no 'consideration' and as such no SDLT is payable even if the value of the extra part of the share is more than the SDLT threshold. HMRC do not need to be advised.

If a property is transferred as a gift again no SDLT will be payable so long as there is no outstanding mortgage; if there is and the transferee takes over payment of some or all of the existing mortgage, then SDLT is due on the value of the mortgage taken over.

Under special rules that apply where property is introduced into a partnership or limited liability partnership the basic principle that SDLT is charged on the amount of the mortgage loan taken over is overridden. In this situation the value for SDLT purposes is equal to whatever proportion of the gross market value is passing out to persons who are not individuals 'connected' with the introducing partner. Spouses and other family members are 'connected' under these rules, and as such there is a nil chargeable consideration for SDLT purposes and therefore no tax payable.

Where chargeable, SDLT is levied such that the percentage rate used applies only to the amount that falls within each band (in a similar way as the charge to income tax applies) except where the home is not the main residence for which 3% is added to each band (but not chargeable if such a property costs less than £40,000 or subject to a long lease). Where a transaction comprises both residential and non residential use then the non residential rates apply to the entire transfer.

## 2020 - 2021 Covid 19 Temporary Increase

As part of the measures to help the economy during the Covid 19 pandemic the Chancellor announced an increase in the SLDT threshold in England and Northern Ireland as from 8 July 2020 to 31 March 2021 which was then extended to 30 June 2021. The nil rate band (NRB) has been temporarily increased from £125,000 to £500,000 producing a saving of up to £15,000 in SDLT for each residential property (although the 3% higher rate for additional dwellings still applies). The band will reduce to £250,000 on 1 September 2021 returning to its normal level of £125,000 as from 1 October 2021.

The first time buyer threshold will return to £300,000 for properties up to £500,000 from 1 July 2021.

The Scottish government also increased the LBTT NRB from £145,000 to £250,000 until 31 March 2021. From 1 April 2021, the threshold reverted back to £145,000. First time buyers benefit from a nil tax threshold of £175,000, as was the position prior to 15 July 2020.

The Welsh government also followed the English government by announcing a temporary increase of LTT for residential property transactions to 30 June 2021. The NRB threshold before 1 July 2021 is £250,000 reverting to £180,000 thereafter. No transitional rules applied.

SDLT rates for properties with a completion date between 1 July 2021 and before 30 September 2021 are:

| Property or lease premium or transfer value | SDLT rate | SDLT rate |
| --- | --- | --- |
|  | Main residence | Second property |
| Up to £250,000 | Zero | 3% |
| The next £675,000 (the portion from £250,001 to £925,000) | 5% | 8% |
| The next £575,000 (the portion from £925,001 to £1.5 million) | 10% | 13% |
| The remaining amount (the portion above £1.5 million) | 12% | 15% |

After 1 October 2021 the rates will revert to:

| Property or lease premium or transfer value | SDLT rate Main residence | SDLT rate Second property |
| --- | --- | --- |
| Up to £125,000 | Zero | 3% |
| The next £125,000 (the portion from £125,001 to £250,000) | 5% | 8% |
| The next £675,000 (the portion from £250,001 to £925,000) | 10% | 13% |
| The next £575,000 (the portion from £925,000 to £1.5 million) | 12% | 15% |
| The remaining amount (the portion above £1.5million) | 15% | 18% |

# 96.   Stamp Duty Land Tax – Companies

The acquisition of a single dwelling by a 'non natural person' is charged to SDLT at a flat rate of 15%. A company is a 'non-natural person' as is a partnership if at least one of the members is a company as well as a collective investment scheme.

There are a number of reliefs that disapply the 15% rate and where a relief is available the normal SDLT rules apply (which may, depending on the circumstances, result in the additional 3% residential rate applying).

To remove a purchase from the 15% regime the dwelling must have been acquired exclusively for any of the following purposes:

- a property rental business where the property is let to unconnected third parties;

- development or redevelopment as part of a property development trade;

- a property trading business;

- for use in a commercially run trade;

- as the business premises of a property rental business;

- for use as a farmhouse by a qualifying farm worker as part of a farming trade;

- for use by an employee for the purposes of a qualifying business;

- for occupation by a caretaker;

- if it is open to the public for at least 28 days per annum.

If the company ceases to hold the property as a business asset within three years of the transfer, then the SDLT originally saved will become payable under a clawback mechanism.

## Stamp Duty Land Tax – Companies

On 1 December 2021 Julie personally buys a commercial rental property valued at £2 million. She wishes to transfer the property into a company where 100% of the shares are owned wholly by her.

Claiming relief from the 15% rate (because the property was to be 'a property rental business where the property is let to unconnected third parties') the SDLT on transfer is charged at the normal SDLT rates i.e.

| Property transfer value | SDLT |
|---|---|
| Up to £125,000 | nil |
| 125,000 x 5% | £ 21,250 |
| £575,000 x 10% | £ 57,500 |
| £500,000 x 12% | £ 60,000 |
| Total SDLT charge | £138,750 |

Had relief not been available (e.g. because Julie intended to live in the property herself), the SDLT charge would have been:

£2million x 15% =£300,000.

Two years later the property becomes vacant and on 31 January 2023 Julie decides to live in the property as her main residence. In this situation, the relief is withdrawn and the amount of SDLT payable on the original transfer is recalculated resulting in a further SDLT charge of £161,250 (i.e. £300,000 - £138,750).

**Note:** An Annual Tax on Enveloped Buildings charge will also be payable once the property has been transferred to the company (see Tip 99).

# 97.   Stamp Duty Land Tax – Multiple Dwellings Relief

'Multiple dwellings relief' (MDR) allows a rate to be charged at the percentage payable on the 'average value' price (referred to as the 'Average Value SDLT' (AVSDLT) should more than one property be purchased at one time, rather than on the total consideration. MDR is only available for residential transactions.

If the relief is claimed, the total SDLT is computed as follows:

1.   Calculate the 'AVSDLT' i.e. total dwellings consideration/ total number of dwellings.

2.   Multiply the resultant figure by the total number of dwellings.

The answer is the total SDLT liability.

**NOTE:** The SDLT must be at least equal to 1% x total dwellings consideration.

In a purchase of four or more dwellings, it might be better not to make an MDR claim but instead classify the transaction as a commercial purchase (depending on the figures).

## Stamp Duty Land Tax - Multiple Dwellings Relief

It is 2 November 2021 and Ben wants to buy flats being offered at a significant discount for bulk purchase. Four flats will cost £700,000 each plus a penthouse flat at £1 million. The transactions are linked.

**Without claiming MDR:**

On each flat: £46,000 ((£125,000 x 3%) + (£125,000 x 5%) + (£450,000 x 8%)).

On penthouse: £73,750 ((£125,000 x 3%) + (£125,000 x 5%) + (£675,000 x 8%) + (£75,000 x 13%)).

Total SDLT charge = £257,750.

With claiming MDR:

Average value = £3.8/5 = £780,000.

AVSDLT = £52,400 ((£125,000 x 3%) + (£125,000 x 5%) + (£530,000 x 8%))).

Total charge = £52,400 x 5 dwellings = £262,000.

Check: SDLT must at least be equal to 1% x total dwellings consideration.

£3.8m x 1% = £38,000.

So, by claiming MDR there is a SDLT extra to pay of £4,250 (£257,750 - £262,000).

## 98.    Stamp Duty Land Tax – Transfer Of 'Connected' Property

If property transactions are linked (e.g. a sale between 'connected' persons), HMRC do not look at each transaction in isolation in order to determine the rate of SDLT to charge; rather, the proceeds are aggregated.

| Stamp Duty Land Tax – Transfer Of 'Connected' Property |
| --- |

On 2 October 2021 John purchases a Buy To Let property for £700,000 – the SDLT charge is calculated:

£125,000 x 0%= £0.00

£125,000 x 8% = £10,000

£450,000 x @ 13% = £58,500

Total £68,500

If the seller arranges a deal whereby the house is sold to John for £650,000 and the garden is sold to John's wife in a separate transaction for £50,000, you might assume that the SDLT liability would amount to £52,000 on John's property only.

However, HMRC link the two transactions together as the two purchasers are 'connected' and SDLT of £68,500 will be payable.

# 99.    Annual Tax On Enveloped Dwellings

The 'Annual Tax on Enveloped Dwellings' (ATED) is an annual charge that was introduced to tackle the avoidance of SDLT by people selling the shares of a company which owned a property rather than the property itself.

Residential properties owned by a 'non-natural' person (generally a company or a partnership with a corporate member or a collective investment scheme, such as a unit trust or an open-ended investment vehicle). Properties valued in excess of £500,000 but less than £1m attract an annual charge of £3,700, the £1m to £2m band properties are charged £7,500 per annum; the bands then increase such that properties valued at over £20m are charged £236,250 (2021/22 rates).

The value of the property for any chargeable period is the later of:

* the date that the property is required or
* the revaluation date

There are fixed revaluation dates for all properties every 5 years after 1 April 2012, e.g. at 1 April 2017, 1 April 2022 etc, regardless of when the property was acquired.

The charge is paid annually in advance by 30 April plus there are in-year filing requirements.

For mixed use properties (i.e. part residential/part non residential) only the residential part is charged. Self-contained flats are valued separately.

If the property has more than one dwelling each owned by a company or someone connected to the company and there is internal access between them or it consists of adjoining buildings with internal access (e.g. two terraced houses) then the property is valued as a single dwelling.

As a UK resident company, gains arising from the property portfolio will normally be subject to 19% Corporation Tax. However, to the extent that such gains are ATED-related, they are specifically excluded from corporation tax and charged to CGT at the higher rate of 28%.

Companies can claim relief from the ATED regime where the property is being let on a commercial basis to third-parties, or where it is being held for property development purposes or where the company's tenant is a shareholder in the company or an associated person of a shareholder. The relief has to be formally claimed.

Relief will be denied if there is any 'non qualifying occupation' which would be the case if an individual connected to the company was permitted to occupy the property or the company is a trading company. When such occupation occurs the relief is withdrawn in respect of that period and usually for any periods preceding and following the occupation until a period of qualifying occupation occurs.

## Annual Tax On Enveloped Dwelling

Justin is the sole shareholder/ director of a company BRT Ltd. The company purchased a buy to let property £1.5 million on 1 April 2021. The annual charge would be £7,500.

An ATED relief declaration was made claiming relief from the charge that would otherwise have applied for the period 1 April 2021 to 31 March 2022 as the intention was for the property to be qualifying.

The property was let out from 1 April 2021 to 30 September 2021. In between tenancies Justin allowed his brother and his wife to stay at the property for one night on 29 November 2021. The property was then let out to tenants as from 1 December 2021.

As occupation had taken place (albeit for one night only) 'non qualifying occupation' had occurred and the relief previously claimed is withdrawn. An amended ATED return is required and £1,253 tax is due.

Calculation for period 1 October 2021 to 30 November 2021:

£7,500/365 x 61 days = £1,253.

## 100.  Value Added Tax – Renovation

If a supply is not zero-rated or exempt, then by default it will be a standard rate (20%) supply. The main difference between zero- rated and exempt supplies is that a business registered for VAT may reclaim/recover all input tax incurred on a zero-rated supply, but no VAT can be reclaimed on exempt supplies.

The one exception to this general rule is with regard to land and property. VAT at a reduced rate of 5% applies to the following types of renovation:

• Conversions of non-residential building into a residential or charitable property.

• Projects where the works refurbish a residential or charitable building that has been empty for two or more years.

• Conversions that change the number of dwellings, e.g. the conversion of one house into flats and conversely, a block of flats back into a single dwelling.

'Residential' includes dwellings (regardless of size), and other residential buildings such as student accommodation. 'Charitable purpose' includes buildings used by charities for non-business purposes such as churches, schools, care homes and day centres.

A special VAT refund scheme allows do-it-yourself (DIY) builders and converters to also recover 5% of the VAT they incurred on construction and conversion costs. The timing of such claims is important as DIY house builders must ensure that claims are submitted within three months of completion of the project. Evidence is needed to support the claim.

## Value Added Tax – Renovation

In May 2019 Adrian purchased a residential bungalow that had not been lived in for a year, intending to convert the property into a house. Planning permission was delayed and not granted until December 2020. Adrian was working on another project at the time and the building work on the bungalow did not start until June 2021. The house was finished in September 2021.

The VAT charges are as follows:

**Purchase of property:** No VAT charge as an exempt supply.

**Renovation work:** As the property had not been lived in for two years or more when the work commenced, the VAT tax charge is 5%. Building materials and certain electrical goods supplied that are incorporated into the building will attract the 5% charge. However, building materials supplied in isolation attract the standard 20% VAT rate.

**Sale of property:** The sale will be exempt from VAT. Should the property have originally been empty for ten years then the VAT charge could be zero-rated.

# 101. Value Added Tax – Developers

VAT-registered developers of new build properties can recover all the VAT charged at the standard 20% VAT rate, as when the building is eventually sold the sale will be charged to VAT albeit at zero-rate.

In recent years some developers have not been able to sell and have had to let out the property instead. VAT on lettings is exempt, therefore in this situation none of the VAT paid can be reclaimed. This is because the builders are deemed to be operating as investors rather than developers.

If VAT has already been reclaimed, then that amount will need to be repaid to HMRC. However, if the new build business comprises a mixture of sold and rented flats then a Partial Exemption calculation will be required to determine the proportion of VAT reclaimable. Normally these costs will be incurred in a year in which there is no income and as such, under the standard VAT claim method, no VAT is reclaimable.

In this situation HMRC will apply a 'de minimus' test using a ten-year economic life in the calculation and thus permit a proportion to be reclaimed, i.e. if the properties are let for one year before being sold, one-tenth of the input VAT would be repaid.

If the 'de minimus' calculation is breached, HMRC will suggest a calculation so that some VAT can be claimed. HMRC's suggestion need not be used and if refused, no VAT can be claimed.

If the property is not a new building, then the sale is likely to be VAT exempt which does not give the right to VAT recovery.

Generally, any pre-existing building needs to cease to exist in order for a claim to be made. However, HMRC's VAT Notice 708 states that if *'the new building makes use of no more than a single facade (or a double facade on a corner site) of a pre-existing building, the pre-existing building is demolished completely (other than the retained facade) before work on the new building is started and the facade is retained as a condition or requirement of statutory planning consent or similar permission'* then they will agree to the supply being zero-rated.

The Notice states that another external wall can be treated as a 'facade' if it is to be retained under the same rules and there is only one facade.

## Value Added Tax – Developers

Julian constructed two properties expecting to sell at £250,000 each.

The input tax recoverable on the building materials was £60,000.

As the properties could not sell it was decided to let instead for a period of three years expecting total rental income from both properties to be £300,000 over the period.

The 'de minimus' calculation is:

£60,000 x 30% = £18,000

HMRC suggest a calculation based on estimated sales values and estimated rents as below:

Estimated eventual sale          x £60,000

Estimated eventual sale plus estimated rents

i.e. <u>£500,000</u>                                    x £60,000

£500,000 + £300,000

This would result in £37,500 of recoverable input VAT, recoverable in the first quarter that Julian decides to let the properties.

If the property had been a corporate development the property could be transferred to that company as a zero-rated supply and as such no 'clawback' of VAT calculation would be required.

# HMRC publications

HMRC provide the following useful products online:

- Live Webinars

If attendance is not possible, a recording is available. There is also a short video that can be viewed on You Tube titled: 'Your income from property - landlords' that shows where property income is declared on a tax return.

- E-Learning Products

HMRC also provides a useful but basic e-learning course specifically for landlords. The system used is a simple intuitive slideshow style.

- Property Rental Toolkit

Toolkits are updated every year and are intended to provide guidance for tax agents and advisers on common errors on tax returns, but they can be viewed by anyone. They comprise a checklist, explanatory notes and links to further guidance. The one of particular relevance to landlords is the one titled: 'Property Rental Toolkit' but the following may also be of interest:

1. Capital Gains Tax for Land and Buildings.

2. Capital v Revenue Expenditure.

3. Inheritance Tax Trusts and Estates.